101
WRESTLING DRILLS
AND GAMES

Keith Manos

ISBN: 1-58518-962-6
Library of Congress Control Number: 2006921121
Book layout: Deborah Oldenburg
Cover design: Studio J Art & Design
Front cover photo: Ross Kinnaird/Getty Images

Coaches Choice
P.O. Box 1828
Monterey, CA 93942
www.coacheschoice.com

Dedication

For my sons—the twins John-Morgan and Christian—who won three matches each by pin or technical fall in their very first wrestling tournament at eight years old. They had to wrestle each other in the finals, and never in my life did I want so desperately for the rules of wrestling to allow a match to end in a tie.

Acknowledgments

To Jim Warstler, a friend, colleague, and fellow coach at Richmond Heights High School, who took the photographs and offered input to the development of this book.

To the wrestlers who demonstrated the drills seen in the photographs:

- Ron Aderhold, a talented junior high wrestler who was 36-4 and second in an Ohio Junior High District Tournament as an eighth grader during the 2004-2005 season
- Brian Connelly, a skilled wrestler for Lake Catholic High School who was 44-7 and fourth at the Ohio High School Division II State Tournament in 2005
- Michael Fee, an outstanding junior high wrestler who was 55-5 and sixth in the Ohio Junior High State Tournament as an eighth grader in 2004-2005.

To Jack Mulhall of Lake Catholic High School, who generously allowed me to use his wrestling room for the photography session.

To Scott Hivnor, coach of the Laker Wrestling Club, who helped arrange the photography session.

To Ben Collado, former head coach at Richmond Heights High School, who offered feedback on the drills featured in this book.

And to Bob Fink, who introduced me to Coaches Choice and Dr. James Peterson.

Thank you all!

Contents

Dedication 3

Acknowledgments 4

Introduction 8

Chapter 1: Warm-Up and Flexibility Drills 11

#1	Jogging in a Circle	#8	Tumbling
#2	Jog and Skip	#9	Bridging
#3	Jog and Swing the Arms ("Rockys")	#10	Push-Ups
#4	Shuffle In/Out	#11	Squats (and Partner Squats)
#5	High Knees	#12	Lifts
#6	Drag the Laces	#13	Inverted Push-Ups
#7	Lunges	#14	Kangaroos

Chapter 2: Agility Drills 25

#15	Jump Rope	#21	Tuck Jumps
#16	Lateral Lunges	#22	Hops
#17	Bear Walk	#23	Limbo
#18	Crab Walk	#24	Hop-Overs
#19	Duck Walks	#25	Break the Tie
#20	Sumo Squats	#26	Partner Turns

Chapter 3: Drills for the Neutral Position—Offense 36

#27	Sumo	#34	Stance and Hand Fight
#28	Stance and Motion	#35	Boundary
#29	Position	#36	Shot/Re-Shot
#30	Lower Level	#37	Wall Shots
#31	Set-Up	#38	Double-Leg Takedown
#32	Tripod—Circle Up	#39	Two Seconds
#33	Fix Position	#40	Sequence Drills

Chapter 4: Drills for the Neutral Position—Defense 52

#41   Sprawl
#42   Hop and Balance
#43   Spin
#44   Bury the Head
#45   Snap and Spin
#46   Prisoners

Chapter 5: Drills for the Top Position 62

#47   Froggy
#48   Spin to Pin
#49   Jam
#50   Pin at the Boundary (Turn His Head)
#51   Float
#52   Wrist and Shift
#53   Kick Him Out
#54   Pin or Kick
#55   30 Seconds
#56   Stand and Single

Chapter 6: Drills for the Bottom Position 71

#57   Hip Heisting
#58   Back-Back
#59   Find the Hands
#60   Post a Foot
#61   Stay Square
#62   Wall Stand-Ups
#63   Pop-Ups
#64   Elevation
#65   Break the Grip
#66   Bridge Him Off
#67   Fight the Nelson
#68   Five Seconds

Chapter 7: Endurance, Stamina and Strength Drills 84

#69   Step-Ups
#70   Relay Races
#71   Weight Class Races
#72   Bleacher Steps
#73   Carry Your Group
#74   Four Corner Sprints
#75   Short Sprints
#76   Push Pop-Ups
#77   Ball Runs
#78   Team Aerobics

Chapter 8: Resistance Training 92

#79   Dumbbell & Barbell Curls
#80   Barbell Squats
#81   Pull-Ups and Chin-Ups
#82   Dips
#83   Bench Press
#84   Upright Row
#85   Rope Climbs
#86   Power Course

Chapter 9: Competitive Wrestling Drills 97

#87   Round Robin Wrestling
#88   One-Minute Matches
#89   Situation Wrestling—Double vs. Sprawl
#90   Situation Wrestling—Single vs. Wizzer

#91   Situation Wrestling—Wrist vs. Belly   #94   Freestyle Wrestling
#92   Situation Wrestling—Back vs. Pin Hold #95   Greco-Roman Wrestling
#93   Shuffle in a Circle and Attack   #96   Counter Wrestling

Chapter 10: Games 107

#97   King of the Mat   #100   Crab Soccer
#98   Touched You Last   #101   Pull Him Out (of the Circle)
#98   Scooter

About the Author. 112

Introduction

This book focuses on fundamental drills every coach can use with his wrestlers so they avoid position mistakes, improve their strength and stamina, and enhance their athleticism. Violating proper position from the neutral, top, or bottom alignments is common among younger wrestlers, so it is crucial that they work diligently and properly when performing these drills. Repetition is also important. Wrestlers are more likely to master a skill and improve their strength and endurance if they are directed to repeat drills daily.

The format of this book is to list the Objective, Location, Description, and special Coaching Points of each drill. The *Objective* refers to the purpose of the drill (why it is important to achievement in a wrestling competition). The wrestlers should be told this purpose each time before beginning the activity. The *Location* indicates where the drill should take place. Coaches may have options here, but most of the drills should be done in the wrestling room for purposes of supervision and safety.

The *Description*, of course, refers to the steps wrestlers should follow to complete the drill. When any drill involves partners—Wrestler A and Wrestler B—it is assumed that Wrestler B has his opportunity to perform the drill once Wrestler A is done. *Coaching Points* are suggestions and comments to highlight for the wrestlers when they are engaged in the drill.

As an overview, throughout all drills the emphasis should be placed on wrestlers having an "attack" attitude (i.e., they constantly pressure their opponents and always look to score from every position). Defensive wrestling, though important to learn, often leads to dull matches and bored fans. Offensive wrestling, however, is fun to teach and exciting to watch.

You need to make clear to your wrestlers that practice must be an active experience. They must be ready each day to hustle throughout the practice and to wrestle (and drill) with intensity. You may even adopt the following format for practice at the beginning of the season.

For the first several weeks, coaches should emphasize wrestling drills and procedures, the building of strength and stamina, and development of technique. A typical practice could have the following schedule:

- Warm-up and agility   20 minutes
- Running   20 minutes
- Weightlifting (2–3 times a week)   25 minutes
- Instruction   40 minutes
- Drilling   35 minutes
- Competitive wrestling   15 minutes

By mid-January, your emphasis should shift to more competitive wrestling and drilling to improve strength and stamina. By this point, most wrestlers have adopted favorite moves and have competed in approximately 12 to 20 matches. Therefore, their training now needs to correct individual mistakes and improve overall conditioning. A typical practice agenda could resemble the following:

- Warm-up and agility   15 minutes
- Running   10 minutes
- Weightlifting (2 times a week)   20 minutes
- Instruction   25 minutes
- Drilling   30 minutes
- Competitive wrestling   45 minutes

By February most squads are preparing in earnest for the postseason tournaments that lead to the State Tournament. At this point, your emphasis should be on avoiding injury, maximizing wrestling skills, and peaking for those tournaments. Practices should be shorter but more intense. To accomplish this objective, coaches could follow the following practice format:

- Warm-up and agility   10 minutes
- Running   10 minutes
- Weightlifting   15 minutes
- Instruction   15 minutes
- Drilling   20 minutes
- Competitive wrestling   50 minutes

Warm-Up and Flexibility Drills

Good flexibility increases a wrestler's ability to avoid injury and move more freely in all directions. Flexibility also makes a wrestler more effective in any "scramble" during a match. In short, significant time spent warming up can mean the difference between health and harm on the mat.

General guidelines for an effective warm-up/flexibility routine include the following tips, which you should share with all of your wrestlers:

- Stretch slowly.

- Avoid bouncing—this ballistic stretching can cause injury and actually tighten muscles.

- Hold each position for 10 to 15 seconds, going from a mild stretch to a more extended stretch (without pain).

- Stretching should not generate pain.

- Concentrate on the muscle or muscles being stretched.

After the initial jogging phase of the warm-up, the team can form a circle with the captain(s) or designated leader(s) in the center. Each exercise and drill is announced by the captain, who then leads the others through the stretch. For example:

Captain: "Butterflies ... Ready?"

Team response: "Yes sir!"

Captain: "Begin!"

Team: "One."

Captain: "Two."

Team: "Three."

Captain: "Four."

Team: "Five." And so on, until the stretch is complete.

This type of dialogue, in which the captain and team alternate numbers, not only sets a serious tone to the warm-up (lending credibility, therefore, to its importance), it also makes all athletes mentally active during the stretch because they have to call out the correct number. Team members remain focused on the stretch while creating a sense of team unity.

Although no time limit should be set, a warm-up is usually 15 to 20 minutes in duration at the beginning of practice. The *minimum* adequate time for effective stretching is 10 minutes. Some individuals could require more than 20 minutes to improve their flexibility, so don't approach the warm-up session with a "let's hurry up and get it over with" attitude

The warm-up period could also serve as a beneficial time to make announcements or establish goals for that practice. Flex your athletes' minds as well as their bodies. At the end of the warm-up they should be stretched, sweating, and prepared to practice.

Drill #1: Jogging in a Circle

Objective: To increase heart rate and the flow of blood to all muscle groups

Location: Wrestling room, gymnasium, or hallway. These laps can be done in the gym or around the perimeter of the mat.

Description: Arrange the team in a circle around the perimeter of the wrestling room, with each wrestler around two to three feet from a teammate. On the whistle, they should start a slow jog while maintaining the circle formation. You can increase or decrease their speed by calling out "sprint," "jog," or "walk" to simulate the sudden explosiveness required in a wrestling match.

Coaching Points:

- Look for wrestlers getting bunched up as faster runners pass slower ones. Direct slower wrestlers to run on the inside and faster ones to run on the outside. Everyone must keep moving.
- If you do this drill in a gymnasium, direct the wrestlers to wear running shoes instead of their wrestling shoes. The gym also provides more room to run and less bunching.

Drill #2: Jog and Skip

Objective: To increase heart rate and the flow of blood to all muscle groups. The muscles also go through an effective transition from an inactive status to an active one.

Location: Wrestling room, gymnasium, track, or hallway

Description: Arrange the team in a circle around the perimeter of the wrestling room or gymnasium, with each wrestler around two to three feet from a teammate. On the whistle, they should start a slow jog, while maintaining the circle formation. At various time intervals (e.g., 15, 30, or 45 seconds), blow the whistle to direct the wrestlers to begin skipping until they hear the whistle again. They can then return to a normal jog.

Coaching Points:

- Be prepared to demonstrate skipping to high school athletes who may have forgotten this activity from their elementary school days.
- Also, expect some comments that skipping is too juvenile. If you do hear complaints, challenge these wrestlers to prove that they can perform a drill they consider childish.

Drill #3: Jog and Swing the Arms ("Rockys")

Objective: To improve cardiovascular conditioning and loosen the muscles in the legs, shoulders, and arms

Location: Wrestling room, gymnasium, or track

Description: Have the wrestlers begin running in a circle while attempting to maintain a three-to-five-foot distance from each teammate. On your command they should begin swinging first the left arm, then the right, and finally both. Tell your athletes to think of Rocky Balboa running in any of the *Rocky* movies. They should begin by swinging their arms in small circular motions horizontally and expand to wider and wider circles as directed.

Coaching Points:

• You can also direct wrestlers to throw short jabs (again, think Rocky Balboa) as they run, but caution them to watch for teammates nearby.

• Be attentive to wrestlers bunching up as they run.

Drill #4: Shuffle In/Out

Objective: To develop techniques to maintain a proper stance while moving the feet laterally and to continue expanding wrestlers' cardiovascular endurance

Location: Wrestling room

Description: Direct wrestlers to get in a circle—facing toward the center—and bend their knees to a square stance position (think football linebacker). On the whistle (or a coach's command) they must begin laterally shuffling in the same direction.

Coaching Point:

- Wrestlers will often bring their feet together as they shuffle, but that defeats the point of the drill. Therefore, remind them throughout the drill to keep their feet separated, their backs vertical, and their butts down.

Drill #5: High Knees

Objective: To increase range of motion in the hips and knees while adding to the stamina of the muscles in these areas

Location: Wrestling room, gymnasium, or hallway

Description: Wrestlers begin on their feet with their arms bent at their sides. On the whistle, they rapidly lift their knees up and down with opposite arm and leg action (i.e., left knee goes up, right arm goes up).

Coaching Points:

- Look for a full extension of the arms and legs.
- The duration of the activity can vary, but the more pumps up and down the better.

Drill #6: Drag the Laces

Objective: To flex the joints in the ankles and knees and effectively stretch the muscles in the groin and legs

Location: Wrestling room

Description: Arrange the wrestlers in a circle around the perimeter of the wrestling mat. They should all be facing in the same direction. Begin with them on both knees and then tell them to take a large step forward while dragging their trailing leg, the laces of their wrestling shoes down toward the mat (i.e., drag the laces). They repeat this process with the other leg and continue around the mat for two to four minutes, extending one leg and then the other.

Coaching Points:

- This drill resembles a penetration step they may use to complete a leg attack takedown. One knee is always down on the mat.

- You also may notice some wrestlers extending their arms left and right to maintain balance. Permit this action at the beginning of the drill, but challenge them to keep their elbows near their sides as they drag their laces around the mat.

Drill #7: Lunges

Objective: To strengthen the leg muscles and increase flexibility in the lower extremities

Location: Wrestling room, gymnasium, or hallway

Description: From a standing position (stance) with the arms bent and forward, wrestlers take a giant step forward with one leg and then return to a stance position. They then repeat this movement with the other leg. See Figure A for the front view and Figure B for a side view.

Coaching Points:

- Be sure wrestlers are separated from each other by five to six feet to prevent them from stepping on each other.
- Remind them to keep their backs in a vertical position (no hunching) and always to have their hands in front of, or above, their lead leg.

Figure A. Front view

Figure B. Side view

Drill #8: Tumbling

Objective: To increase the flexibility of the shoulders while loosening up the joints and muscles in the arms and upper torso. Tumbling activities also add to mat awareness and help to increase an athlete's range of motion in the hips, knees, and ankles.

Location: Wrestling room

Description: Place the wrestlers in equal lines at one end of the mat and direct them to do forward rolls and backward rolls. Remind them to tuck the chin toward the chest and to maintain momentum in a straight line.

Once they show competency with the basic forward and backward rolls, have them attempt dives into a forward roll and backward extensions. The dive into a forward roll begins with the wrestler in his stance. He takes a few short steps forward, pushes off his feet, and dives head first with the arms extended toward the mat. Once his palms hit the mat, he bends his arms to cushion his fall and tucks his head to begin the forward roll.

To perform backward extensions, after leaning back for a basic backward roll, the wrestler puts his hands at his shoulders with the palms toward the mat. He then pushes off his hands, extends his arms and legs straight to the ceiling, and lands on his feet to complete the drill.

Coaching Point:

- Some heavier wrestlers (or those with below-average upper-body strength) may struggle to complete the backward extensions.

Drill #9: Bridging

Objective: To increase the range of motion in the shoulders and neck while adding to the stamina of the muscles in these areas. Moreover, this drill emphasizes that getting pinned is a wrestler's worst insult. Even a champion can find himself suddenly caught on his back. If it does happen, all wrestlers need to know how to get off their backs quickly and into a better position to escape.

Location: Wrestling room

Description: Wrestlers begin on their backs and place the crown of their heads on the mat. Using the neck muscles, they then bridge off the mat, slide one elbow underneath them, go to a tripod position (the three points being the two feet and the hands, which are positioned together on the mat), and circle up to their feet. Figure A shows a front bridge and Figure B shows a back bridge.

Coaching Point:

* Bridging effectively and bridging to a hip heist are crucial skills for a successful wrestler. It may seem unfortunate to have to teach this skill, but this drill must be done often, preferably daily.

Figure A. Front bridge

Figure B. Back bridge

Drill #10: Push-Ups

Objective: To increase energy levels and improve muscle endurance in the shoulders and arms

Location: Wrestling room, gymnasium, or hallway

Description: Wrestlers begin with their chests, pelvic area, and legs flat on the mat (or floor), then push up, keeping their backs level and parallel with the floor. Vary the drill by changing the position of their hands—close, shoulder-width, wide—or their feet (elevating them on a partner's back or a bench).

Coaching Point:

- Push-ups are one of the oldest and most common strength-building exercises for athletes.

Drill #11: Squats (and Partner Squats)

Objective: To strengthen the joints and muscles of the hips, legs, and lower back

Location: Wrestling room, gymnasium, or hallway

Description: From a wrestling stance position (think football linebacker), wrestlers bend at the knees and squat, as if sitting in a chair. The arms should be bent with the elbows tight to the sides, and the back should be vertical and the head up.

Coaching Points:

- Wrestlers must maintain good stances as they squat.
- You could increase the challenge of the drill by making them squat with a partner of equal or greater weight on their back. See photo for the partner squat.

Drill #12: Lifts

Objective: To strengthen the joints and muscles of the hips, legs, and back. Wrestlers can also gain endurance in their shoulder and arm muscles. This exercise also duplicates the skills required for finishing a high crotch or outside single takedown.

Location: Wrestling room

Description: Wrestler A places his head behind Wrestler B's armpit with one arm tight around his waist and the other arm elbow deep in the crotch from behind. On the whistle, Wrestler A then squats, hips in, and lifts Wrestler B (holding for several seconds). On the second whistle, Wrestler A returns Wrestler B gently to the mat. Wrestler A and Wrestler B should then change positions.

As the wrestlers develop skill here, coaches can vary the return to the mat, as if finishing the high crotch or outside single leg takedown. See photo.

Coaching Points:

* Note how well Wrestler A brings his hips in tight to his partner while maintaining control with one arm around the waist and the other around the leg (thigh). Caution him not to lean back.

* Be sure that the wrestlers are separated by a safe distance.

* Make sure you demonstrate how to safely return Wrestler B to the mat.

Drill #13: Inverted Push-Ups

Objective: To build strength in the arms and shoulders and increase the endurance of the muscles in the upper body. This drill enables wrestlers to add power to any technique.

Location: Wrestling room

Description: The wrestlers are upside down, with their feet above their heads and against the wall and their arms supporting their body. Have them face away from the wall as they lower and lift (i.e., push up) their body. Direct them to do a certain number of repetitions or to continue pushing up and down for a pre-set amount of time.

Coaching Point:

- Heavier wrestlers typically struggle, first just to get their legs above their heads, and second to push their heads off the mat. Therefore, be especially observant of their efforts in this activity.

Drill #14: Kangaroos

Objective: To strengthen the legs and add endurance to the thigh and calf muscles. The drill also duplicates in part a plyometric exercise to prompt explosiveness out of a typical stance.

Location: Wrestling room

Description: Place wrestlers either in lines or in a circle facing the same direction. They should be in a square stance with their feet positioned shoulder-width apart and their legs bent at the knees (no bending at the waist). See photo for the starting position. On the whistle, the wrestlers should spring (i.e., hop) forward off the balls of their feet and land back in a stance position, ready to push off again.

Coaching Point:

- Caution wrestlers about straightening up after they spring forward. They should maintain a stance position (back straight, head up, legs and arms bent) throughout the drill. As they tire, they may start to hop and land on straight legs, so remind them to maintain bent legs and a straight back.

2

Agility Drills

These drills, whether done individually or with partners, are designed to improve wrestlers' overall agility, strength, and speed. They should be performed after the warm-up and before any type of competitive wrestling. Always stress the importance of hustling during each drill and look for improvement from week to week.

Although some of these drills are not wrestling-specific—that is, they do not duplicate specific wrestling techniques or maneuvers—they do build strength in the specific muscle groups needed to complete wrestling moves. Therefore, wrestlers must complete them properly without stopping, maintain good form, and cooperate with partners when necessary.

Overall, the key is to keep these brief agility drills fun and lively. Coaches should want their wrestlers to show improvement in both skill and energy level. Make sure they know the format and structure of each drill before beginning, and remind them that an agility drill may also be an aerobic activity.

Agility Drills—Individual

Drill #15: Jump Rope

Objective: To develop stamina and endurance in the shoulders, legs, and arms. This drill also improves an athlete's cardiovascular conditioning.

Location: Wrestling room, gymnasium, or hallway

Description: Be sure each wrestler is at least six to 10 feet away from teammates when he is jumping rope. Coaches can change the duration (10, 20, 30, 60 seconds), speed (a slow pace to as fast as possible), and movement (double jumps, walk the rope, hop on one foot) of the rope jumping. As the wrestlers' skill progresses, you may even challenge them with cross-over jumps and reverse rope jumping.

Coaching Point:

- Jump ropes come in various lengths. Taller and larger wrestlers will need longer jump ropes to complete this drill.

Drill #16: Lateral Lunges

Objective: To improve flexibility in the groin, hips, and legs, and to increase endurance and strength in the thigh muscles

Location: Wrestling room, gymnasium, or hallway

Description: From a standing position, wrestlers should first step the right foot two feet to the right and bend the right knee, keeping the head up, the back as straight as possible, the arms bent, and the toes forward. They then return to a standing position and repeat with the left leg.

Coaching Points:

- Be sure that the wrestlers maintain a safe distance from teammates and keep their balance as they lunge right and left.
- Heavier wrestlers may not be able to lunge as far or bend their knees as much.

Drill #17: Bear Walk

Objective: To strengthen the muscles in the shoulders, arms, hips, and legs. This drill in part mimics wrestling maneuvers from the bottom position.

Location: Wrestling room

Description: Position wrestlers either in lines or in a circle with their hands and the balls of their feet on the mat. Both the arms and legs should be slightly bent and the head must be up. See photo for the proper position. On the whistle, wrestlers should move forward while under control and maintaining this position. This exercise is not a speed drill. Control is the key.

Coaching Points:

- You can expand this drill to include wrestlers moving right, left, and backward.
- You could also do this drill in a hallway or gym, but be careful about the wrestlers' hands on the hard surface.

Drill #18: Crab Walk

Objective: To strengthen the shoulder, arm, and leg muscles. This drill also mimics a common bottom position for wrestlers.

Location: Wrestling room

Description: Arrange wrestlers either in lines or a circle, in the crab position, with their palms and feet flat on the mat. Their backs should be straight up and down, their hips beneath their shoulders, and their heads up. See photo for the proper position. On the whistle, direct them to move forward. This exercise is not a speed drill. Their goal is to maintain this position as they move.

Coaching Points:

- Caution wrestlers about extending themselves in this drill. That is, remind them to keep their hips beneath their shoulders and avoid letting the hips drift toward the feet.

- You can also have wrestlers move left, right, and backward. Eventually, direct them to perform a hip heist action from this position.

Drill #19: Duck Walks

Objective: To strengthen the legs and hips and increase flexibility in both muscle groups

Location: Wrestling room, gymnasium, or hallway

Description: Position wrestlers either in lines or a circle and direct them to squat, keeping the back straight but slightly forward, the head up, and the butt about one foot off the mat or floor. They should bend their arms and place their elbows close to their knees.

Coaching Point:

- Some wrestlers may attempt this drill using the surfboard technique, which has them positioned with their arms wide and extended for balance. Eventually, however, they should get their arms tight to their sides.

Drill #20: Sumo Squats

Objective: To increase flexibility in the legs and strengthen the thigh muscles. Maintaining a strong stance in the neutral position throughout a match is difficult for wrestlers who cannot keep their legs bent at the knees and move in various directions. This drill mimics the bent-knee/flexed-leg position required of wrestlers in the neutral position.

Location: Wrestling room, gymnasium, or hallway

Description: Wrestlers begin by standing with the feet positioned somewhat wider than shoulder width and their toes pointed slightly out. On the whistle, they should squat (like a sumo wrestler), flaring the knees out and keeping their elbows inside their knees. Their heels should be flat to the mat or floor. Wrestlers can repeat the sumo squat on their own or on the whistle.

Coaching Point:

- Caution wrestlers about leaning too far forward as they squat (their backs should not be hunched).

Drill #21: Tuck Jumps

Objective: To develop explosiveness from all positions—neutral, top, and bottom. This drill also improves leg strength and overall conditioning.

Location: Wrestling room, gymnasium, or hallway

Description: The wrestlers begin in a standing position. On the whistle, the wrestlers jump, bringing both knees to the chest in a tuck position. They should keep their backs as straight as possible, avoiding hunching over the knees. They should perform the next jump as soon as they land.

Coaching Point:

- Some wrestlers may tire quickly and rest for several seconds between jumps. Encourage them to continue the drill as instructed to mimic the explosiveness necessary in a wrestling match.

Drill #22: Hops

Objective: To improve leg strength and endurance in the ankles and knees. This drill can also improve a wrestler's level of conditioning.

Location: Wrestling room, gymnasium, or hallway

Description: The wrestlers begin in a standing position. On the whistle, wrestlers hop in the direction designated by the coach, bringing both feet six to eight inches off the mat or floor. They should keep their backs as straight as possible, avoiding hunching over at the waist. They should perform the next hop as soon as they land on one foot. Be sure to perform this drill with both the right and left foot.

Coaching Points:

- Coaches can have the wrestlers hop forward, backward, or laterally. They could also hop only on the right or left foot. Finally, coaches could have wrestlers "chop" their feet in the same place, if desired.

- Some wrestlers may tire quickly and rest for several seconds between hops. Encourage them to continue the drill as instructed to mimic the explosiveness necessary in a wrestling match.

Agility Drills—Partners

Drill #23: Limbo

Objective: To lower the level on leg attacks and improve the penetration step motion

Location: Wrestling room, gymnasium, or hallway

Description: Wrestler B stands and extends one arm laterally right or left from his body at various heights. Wrestler A must bend at the knees, keep his back as straight as possible and his head up, and then step beneath the extended arm of Wrestler B, as if doing the limbo but without leaning back (see Figures A and B). After several repetitions, the wrestlers should reverse positions.

Coaching Point:

- Watch for wrestlers simply ducking (i.e., bending at the waist) beneath the extended arm and not bending at the knees. As Wrestler A gains proficiency, have Wrestler B lower the height of his extended arm.

Figure A

Figure B

Drill #24: Hop-Overs

Objective: To increase leg strength while increasing flexibility in the ankles and knees. This drill also should help wrestlers recognize the importance of power and speed for completing takedown techniques.

Location: Wrestling room, gymnasium, or hallway

Description: Wrestler B maintains a prone position (e.g., a semi-push-up position). On the whistle, Wrestler A hops from side to side. Wrestler A's feet should be about a foot apart at the beginning and end of each hop-over. He should keep hopping until he hears the whistle.

Coaching Points:

- During this drill, Wrestler B can shift his position from a prone position to almost a base position, which makes the drill more challenging and increases the stamina Wrestler A's legs.

- Wrestler A should maintain a proper stance throughout the drill.

Drill #25: Break the Tie

Objective: To teach techniques to prevent an opponent from controlling the head in the neutral position and to encourage constant motion on the feet

Location: Wrestling room

Description: Wrestler B begins with a collar/head tie-up on Wrestler A. Both wrestlers should be in good stances. On the whistle, Wrestler A uses his hand (thumb up) to push Wrestler B's tie-up arm *in* (at the elbow), and circles away. Wrestler A must keep his head up at all times and circle away toward the side of the tie-up (i.e., if Wrestler A pushes with his right hand, he circles left). See Figures A and B.

Coaching Point:

- This drill mimics a common situation for wrestlers in the neutral position. Remind wrestlers not to dip or lower their heads to get their opponent's hand off their neck when breaking off the opponent's tie-up.

Figure A. Starting position

Figure B. Finishing position

Drill #26: Partner Turns

Objective: To expand overall body strength, especially for the muscles in the legs, back, and arms. This drill also mimics the kind of motion a wrestler could use when lifting an opponent and returning him to the mat.

Location: Wrestling room

Description: Wrestler B assumes a position on all fours (feet and knees on the mat). Wrestler A stands to the side. On the whistle, Wrestler A bear hugs Wrestler B around his waist, squats, lifts, and then turns Wrestler B so that Wrestler B's head faces in the opposite direction. See Figures A, B, and C. The movement should be quick and efficient.

Coaching Point:

• Pair wrestlers in the same weight class. If, however, the heavier wrestlers cannot lift one another, allow them to lift a lighter teammate.

Figure A. Starting position

Figure B. The lift

Figure C. Final position

3

Drills for the Neutral Position—Offense

Wrestlers have to be encouraged to be offensive, push their opponents, and attack from all directions. In the neutral position, they should move in short, choppy steps and attack only after gaining contact and an angle on the opponent. Fast hands plus fast feet usually equals success in gaining takedowns.

Proper position, of course, is also very important. The repetition of the following fundamental drills can help wrestlers identify proper position and regain it whenever they are caught out of position.

For many of these drills, Wrestler A and Wrestler B should be matched according to weight class and skill level. Most drills begin with Wrestler A performing the drill first before switching positions with Wrestler B, though some drills are performed in unison.

The drills here should be done at various speeds—half, three-quarters—with Wrestler B serving as a functional drill partner for Wrestler A. Coaches may have to demonstrate the intensity of the resistance for the wrestlers so that the drills can be performed accurately. Indeed, teaching *how* to drill is often as important as the drill itself.

Before engaging wrestlers in any of these drills, which are more specific to actual wrestling techniques, you should introduce some important concepts to your athletes:

- How to drill (the buddy system)
- Training for mastery
- Avoiding illegal holds and techniques
- Acting vs. reacting
- Stance, motion, set up, and penetration—attacking on contact
- Knowing when to attack and when not to
- Moving in a series
- Having mat awareness
- Never chasing an opponent in the neutral position
- Attacking low and high stances

Wrestlers must know how to train effectively with a drill partner and get in top condition. They should understand proper position, various set-ups, and the offensive and defensive maneuvers from all neutral situations. They must recognize the importance of aggressive wrestling, moving in a series, and positioning themselves in advantageous alignments.

You may choose to proceed at a faster or slower rate and, in fact, teach different techniques. But remember, teaching a few moves thoroughly is better than covering many moves briefly. After the third week of practice and the first match, the coaching staff should evaluate strengths and weaknesses and then plan the following week's practices to deal with those areas that require improvement.

The following are the final keys to the drills and skills associated with wrestling in the neutral position:

- Make sure the wrestlers can accomplish the drill appropriately for their age and skill-level.
- Ensure that enough time is provided to accomplish the drill.
- Be sure wrestlers are clear about the objective of the drill.
- Begin the drill slowly and then pick up the speed.

Drill #27: Sumo

Objective: To improve stance, motion, and upper-body agility in the neutral position

Location: Wrestling room

Description: In good stances, Wrestlers A and B face each other, chest on chest, with their hands on each other's shoulders and chins against each other's shoulders. They must lean into each other, but not push or pull with their hands or arms. See photo for the correct starting position. On the whistle, each wrestler tries to use his upper body to move his partner backward, left, or right by moving their legs and shoving with their chests.

Coaching Point:

- Typically, the wrestler who can maintain good position is the one who keeps moving his feet and stays focused on a proper stance. When wrestlers only push—without moving their feet—they are more likely to lose balance.

Drill #28: Stance and Motion

Objective: To teach a proper stance (head up and forward, back straight, legs and arms bent, and feet an inch or two wider than shoulder-width apart)

Location: Wrestling room

Description: On the whistle, the wrestlers should go from an upright, relaxed position to a proper stance in which their legs are bent at the knees, their arms are bent at the elbows and close to their sides, their heads are up and forward (tell them to get their chins over their toes), and their hands in front of their midsection with the fingers curled. On the second whistle, they must begin moving their feet in various directions—forward, laterally, back—all the while maintaining the proper stance.

Coaching Points:

- Be sure wrestlers are positioned five to eight feet apart to prevent them from bumping into each other.
- Caution them about sliding their feet on the mat instead of stepping, and remind wrestlers to move in all directions—forward, backward, and laterally.

Drill #29: Position

Objective: To teach wrestlers how to maintain a proper stance—legs bent, back straight, arms bent with the elbows tight to the body (to deny underhooks), head up and forward, and hands in front of the body to oppose pressure from an opponent

Location: Wrestling room

Description: Wrestler A assumes a proper wrestling stance (refer to Drill #28). On the whistle, Wrestler B pushes him (with the hands at his shoulders, chest, or head), pulls him (grabbing the arms or head), and/or twists him to get Wrestler A off balance. Wrestler A must resist by keeping his feet moving and using his hands to aggressively counter the actions of Wrestler B until he hears the next whistle.

Coaching Point:

- Caution wrestlers about dipping or lowering their heads (i.e., face toward the mat) to counter Wrestler B's efforts to move their heads. The head must stay up with the eyes on the opponent at all times. The key is to move with choppy steps and to avoid leaning forward or getting extended (i.e., straightening the legs and arms).

Drill #30: Lower Level

Objective: To develop techniques to properly initiate a leg attack. Wrestlers need to learn to lower their level by bending the legs instead of the waist (and lunging at an opponent) when shooting at the opponent's legs.

Location: Wrestling room

Description: Wrestlers must learn the level change technique from a staggered stance position (i.e., one foot is slightly ahead of the other in their stance). On the whistle, the wrestlers bend the knees, lower the midsection, and step the lead foot (the foot closest to the opponent) four to six inches forward. This drill can be done either against a padded wall or a stationary partner. Wrestlers do not need to complete an actual leg attack.

Coaching Points:

- Lowering the level is crucial to any successful leg attack. Caution wrestlers about simply bending at the waist instead of at the knees and lunging at the drill partner (or opponent).

- Add the penetration step after wrestlers have mastered lowering their level. A strong penetration step is the next link in any leg attack. Wrestlers should step only eight to 12 inches (any farther could put them off-balance), bend their knees, and drive the hips forward. When they make contact with the wall or the partner, they must have their hips beneath them, and the trailing foot cannot pass the down knee.

Figure A. Starting position   Figure B. Final position

Drill #31: Set-Up

Objective: To improve wrestlers' opportunities for achieving a leg-attack takedown

Location: Wrestling room

Description: Wrestler B acts as a good drill partner as Wrestler A uses various set-ups to get Wrestler B out of good position and open for a leg attack. Action should begin and stop on the whistle and then positions should be reversed.

• Drive the Car—Wrestler A places his palms on Wrestler B's biceps—inside control—as if gripping a car's steering wheel. Wrestler A keeps his elbows in and stays in a good stance as he "turns the wheel" to move Wrestler B's arms away from his legs (see Figure A).

• Head Tie and Wrist—Wrestler A grips Wrestler B's head (collar) with one hand and Wrestler B's opposite wrist or hand with his other hand. As Wrestler A pulls or pushes with the head tie hand he should lift or extend Wrestler B's arm with his other hand (see Figure B).

• Underhook—Wrestler A underhooks Wrestler B on one side and controls Wrestler B's opposite bicep, wrist, or hand with his other hand. With the underhook arm, Wrestler A tugs, pulls, and shoves Wrestler B out of a good position while pulling and extending the opposite arm of Wrestler B.

Coaching Point:

• Constant motion with the feet is especially important for an effective set-up. Wrestlers cannot stop, do a set up, and then move—all actions must be simultaneous.

Figure A. Drive the car

Figure B. Head tie and wrist

Drill #32: Tripod—Circle Up

Objective: To instruct on how to complete a stalled inside single-leg attack

Location: Wrestling room

Description: Place the wrestlers in a tripod position with their weight on the balls of each foot and the hands close together beneath the face (see Figure A). On the whistle or coach's command, the wrestlers circle either to the left or right depending on the imaginary opponent in front of them. As they circle up in short steps, they must suck the hands in toward the stomach, pulling in the imaginary leg (see Figures B and C).

Coaching Points:

- Your first command could be "tripod," which tells each wrestler to place his hands together on the mat in front of him and come off his knees so his body forms a tripod (hands, left foot, right foot). On your next command of "circle up," he uses choppy steps in one direction and circles up into a good stance, pulling his hands tight to his stomach as if to pull in the imaginary leg.

- Be sure the wrestlers have their heads up and are separated by at least five feet. Also, the arms and legs should always remain bent.

Figure A. Starting position

Figure B. Wrestlers begin to circle up

Figure C. Final position

Drill #33: Fix Position

Objective: To teach wrestlers how to recover from poor positions after attempting a leg attack—like a stalled single leg. The two versions of this drill duplicate what any wrestler could face in an actual match.

Location: Wrestling room

Description: Two versions of this drill should be performed.

• Fix Position—One Knee Down: Wrestlers assume a position in which one knee is on the mat, one foot is planted parallel to that knee, the back is straight, and the head is up (see Figure A). On the whistle, wrestlers push off the planted foot and circle up in the opposite direction (e.g., if the right knee is down and the left foot is planted, they push off the left foot and circle up to the right). They should pretend to be pulling in an imaginary leg (see Figure B).

• Fix Position—Two Knees Down: Begin the drill with all wrestlers on both knees with the back straight and head up. On the whistle, they step up with one foot, plant that foot on the mat, push off of it, and circle up in the opposite direction (e.g., if the wrestler plants his right foot, he pushes off of it and circles up to his left). The wrestler should pretend to pull in an imaginary leg.

Coaching Points:

• This drill resembles what often happens with a stalled single leg attack—that is, when a wrestler attacks a single leg and gets stopped by a sprawl or hip down technique. Wrestlers need to know how to fix their position and finish the single leg attack.

• Later, coaches can put wrestlers with partners, and have Wrestler A place his hands inside and next to one knee of Wrestler B. On the whistle or coach's command Wrestler A grips the leg of Wrestler B circles up with Wrestler B's leg.

Figure A

Figure B

Drill #34: Stance and Hand Fight

Objective: To duplicate actual face-to-face situations in which both wrestlers attempt to maneuver their opponents out of position and make them vulnerable to attack. The goal for the wrestlers is twofold: stay in good position and get the opponent out of a good stance.

This drill forces both wrestlers to focus on proper stance and motion while under constant pressure from an opponent. Wrestlers need to work at both giving and countering pressure in the neutral position. Wrestlers need to prepare for opponents who come at them from a variety of stances and directions.

Location: Wrestling room

Description: Wrestlers A and B square off, facing each other in good stances. On the whistle, they simultaneously try to shove, jostle, and pull each other out of position. They should be aggressive with their hands and stay in constant motion. Both must sustain constant, forward, and aggressive movement.

Coaching Points:

- Caution wrestlers especially about backing up or avoiding contact. Also, remind them to shift directions; they do not have to keep going forward and backward during this drill.
- After the wrestlers have either shown competency or sluggishness with this drill, add some variables, including starting with Wrestlers A and B in different positions. Of course, they do not stay in those positions. If back to back or side to side, they will quickly turn and face off. If kneeling, they will certainly step up to their feet. These variations add a little more difficulty and change the routine of this basic wrestling drill.
    - ✓ Back to back
    - ✓ Left side to left side
    - ✓ One kneeling vs. one standing
    - ✓ Both kneeling

Drill #35: Boundary

Objective: To teach techniques to move an opponent away from the boundary so an offensive attack does not end up going out of bounds. When confronted by an opponent who plays the edge of the mat, wrestlers need to know how to move him away from the boundary and open him up for a takedown attempt.

Location: Wrestling room

Description: Wrestler A squares off against Wrestler B, whose back and heels are only one foot away from the boundary (use the practice circles or the out-of-bounds line on the actual mat). On the whistle, Wrestler A takes choppy steps to the left or right in a circular pattern, angling his position to the boundary line and circling Wrestler B away from the edge. After several repetitions from both sides, the wrestlers should reverse positions.

Coaching Point:

• Coaches can add elements of the Stance and Hand Fight (Drill #34) to this drill as well.

Drill #36: Shot/Re-Shot

Objective: To emphasize the penetration step and take advantage of an opponent's poor position to complete a leg attack

Location: Wrestling room

Description: First, review how to lower the level and take a penetration step. Then have Wrestler B take a poor shot against Wrestler A, who sprawls, forcing Wrestler B to put his hands on the mat and back out. As Wrestler B backs out and straightens himself, Wrestler A lowers his level and takes a penetration step (i.e., re-shot) for a leg attack of his choice. Reverse positions after several attempts.

Coaching Point:

• Begin the drill slowly and increase the speed only after the wrestlers have mastered lowering their level and penetrating. Wrestler A must stay under control and be balanced. You do not want one poor shot followed by another.

Drill #37: Wall Shots

Objective: To teach wrestlers to take a proper penetration step, keep their heads up, and maintain balance when hitting a double-leg takedown.

Location: Wrestling room

Description: The wrestlers face the wall (hopefully a padded one) in a staggered stance position (i.e., with one foot slightly ahead of the other) (see Figure A). On the whistle, each wrestler must lower his level, step toward the wall with the lead foot until his knee touches the mat right before the wall, and drive his chest to the wall, dragging the trailing leg forward. The wrestlers should end with their palms on the wall in front of their chests (see Figure B).

Coaching Point:

- Be sure that the wrestlers are neither too close nor too far away from the wall when doing this drill. Allow them the first several attempts to experiment with the proper distance.

Figure A. Starting position

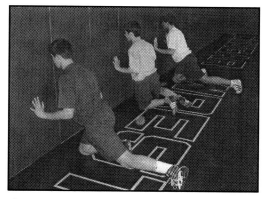

Figure B. Final position

Drill #38: Double-Leg Takedown

Objective: To improve double-leg takedown technique, while also improving endurance in the leg, back, and arm muscles

Location: Wrestling room

Description: Place the wrestlers in lines. Wrestler A begins in the first stage of a double-leg takedown, on his knees with his arms around Wrestler B's legs, his hands behind Wrestler B's knees, his head tight to the side of Wrestler B, his chest against Wrestler B's thighs, and one knee down splitting Wrestler B's legs (see Figure A). On the whistle, Wrestler A allows Wrestler B to sprawl a little bit and then scoots forward and pulls Wrestler B's legs toward him again (see Figure B). They continue this drill down the length of the mat. Once the pair reaches the edge of the mat, they should reverse their positions.

Coaching Point:

* Watch for wrestlers dipping their heads toward the mat or extending their backs until they are more like table tops instead of waterfalls. They must maintain proper upper-body position as they move on their knees down the mat.

Figure A. Starting position

Figure B. Wrestler A scoots forward and pulls Wrestler B towards him

Drill #39: Two Seconds

Objective: To teach wrestlers to attack an opponent quickly and aggressively approximately two seconds after the official blows his whistle

Location: Wrestling room

Description: Within two seconds after hearing the whistle, Wrestler A must make contact with Wrestler B by using a set-up followed by a leg or upper-body attack. The drill simulates a situation in which little time is left in a period or in which Wrestler A is attempting to force Wrestler B to backpedal and potentially get called for stalling.

Coaching Points:

- Head, hand, and foot fakes are important in this drill. Also, when rushing to attack an opponent, it is not uncommon for wrestlers to neglect a set-up and/or a penetration step and simply lunge at the opponent. The purpose of the drill is to prompt aggressiveness, while not allowing sloppy offensive attacks. While quickness is an important element of the drill, the wrestlers must still show proper position and technique as they work to catch an opponent off guard.

Drill #40: Sequence Drills

Objective: To practice a variety of offensive techniques from the neutral position. This drill empowers wrestlers to think about attempting various takedown techniques, possibly in succession. They can make easier transitions from one maneuver to the next and become more conscious of planning several moves in advance. When sequence drilling, wrestlers are always moving and attempting various takedowns.

Location: Wrestling room

Description: In selected practice circles, place index cards with the names of takedown techniques (double-leg, single-leg, high crotch, fireman's carry, duck under, etc.). On the whistle, wrestlers take turns hitting that takedown maneuver. On the next whistle, they move to the next circle and do that takedown. The drill continues until all pairs have attempted all of the takedowns.

Coaching Points:

- It is important that wrestlers use motion, a set up, good penetration, and a strong finish at every station.
- The wrestlers in each pairing should have an equal number of attempts at each technique.

4

Drills for the Neutral Position—Defense

Although many coaches advocate offensive wrestling—both to score points and promote aggressiveness—defensive wrestling and the drills needed to teach defensive wrestling cannot be neglected. These drills can help wrestlers who are not as quick or agile score points and take advantage of an opponent's poor offensive technique.

Drill #41: Sprawl

Objective: To prompt wrestlers to get the knees back, hips down, and the weight onto the shoulders of an opponent after he shoots at their legs. Countering an opponent's quick leg attack is vital in any wrestling match. Every wrestler should be prepared to turn a defensive maneuver into a scoring opportunity.

Location: Wrestling room

Description: Be sure that the wrestlers are spread out so that they have at least six to eight feet between them to prevent them from falling onto each other. Each wrestler should begin in a predetermined stance, for example, a staggered stance left foot lead or a staggered stance right foot lead (see Figure A). On the whistle, the wrestlers must throw the hips down and the knees and feet back, falling onto their forearms where their feet originally were positioned (see Figure B).

The legs should remain flexed and wide, and the hands should be ready to pressure the imaginary opponent's head and arms. Finish the drill by having the wrestlers circle up into their stances, ready to sprawl again.

Coaching Point:

- Caution wrestlers who simply fall to their bellies and do not keep their heads up that they must fall to their forearms and keep their chest off the mat.

Figure A. Starting position

Figure B. Final position

Drill #42: Hop and Balance

Objective: To develop techniques to maintain balance and pressure against an opponent who sweeps a leg off the mat. When caught by a single-leg attack during which a leg gets elevated, a wrestler needs to recover from this potential scoring opportunity for his opponent.

Location: Wrestling room

Description: Begin the drill with the offensive man (Wrestler B) already in control with a single leg off the mat (see Figure A). On the whistle, the offensive wrestler shoves and pushes the defensive man, Wrestler A, around the practice circle, forcing him to hop on one foot. After eight to 10 seconds of hopping, a coach should then shout "Counter!" which is the command for Wrestler A to do the following:

- Grab the elbows of the offensive man (or one wrist and use a wizzer)
- Hip in with the hip closest to the offensive man
- Move the foot that is off the mat outside the near leg of the offensive wrestler
- Shove the up foot to the mat hard (see Figure B)
- Circle away from Wrestler B and into a good stance (see Figure C)

Coaching Points:

- Wrestler A must pull up on Wrestler B's elbows to lock out his arms and pressure them off the leg he's holding. Circling away at the end of the technique is also very important. If the defensive wrestler stays near the offensive wrestler, he risks having his leg simply grabbed again.
- Have the wrestlers switch positions after each repetition.

Figure A. Starting position

Figure B. Wrestler A wizzers hard and drives his foot to the mat.

Figure C. Wrestler A circles away and squares off against Wrestler B.

Drill #43: Spin

Objective: To practice the correct hip movement when spinning behind an opponent after his poor leg attack. This drill can also serve as an excellent conditioning drill.

Location: Wrestling room

Description: Position Wrestler B on all fours (knees and hands on the mat) and Wrestler A with his chest on Wrestler B's shoulders and his hands on Wrestler B's upper body. Wrestler A must also have his legs flexed, his arms bent, and his head up. See photo. On the whistle, Wrestler A begins spinning around Wrestler B's body in short, choppy steps. As he spins, he should push down on Wrestler B's head and in on his arms at the elbow. The coach can use the whistle or more commands to switch the direction of Wrestler A's spinning.

Coaching Points:

- It is common for wrestlers to neglect pushing down on the head or in on the arms as they spin, so keep reminding them throughout the drill. It is important that they perform these actions to prevent Wrestler B from simply blocking the spin by raising an arm to the left or right.

- You can increase the complexity of the drill by having Wrestler B slowly move in various directions on his hands and knees as Wrestler A continues spinning.

Drill #44: Bury the Head

Objective: To teach techniques to prevent offensive wrestlers from completing a leg attack

Location: Wrestling room

Description: Begin with Wrestler B in a simulated double-leg position with his head tight to the hip of Wrestler A. Wrestler A must be squared off against him in a semi-sprawl (see Figure A). On the whistle, Wrestler A shoves Wrestler B's head beneath his stomach and pressures the upper torso of Wrestler B with his hips and chest (see Figure B). Wrestler B then continually tries to get his head out and to the side of Wrestler A.

Coaching Points:

- Wrestler A's hand should be on the crown of Wrestler B's head when he shoves the head beneath his stomach. Look for Wrestler A to have proper hip pressure on Wrestler B, along with flexed legs.

- Have the wrestlers switch positions after each repetition.

Figure A

Figure B

Drill #45: Snap and Spin

Objective: To combine the Sprawl and Spin drills (Drills #41 and #43) into one technique that can be used in competition when an opponent shoots poorly at the legs

Location: Wrestling room

Description: Wrestler B takes a poor (50 to 60%) shot at Wrestler A, who sprawls, shoves down on Wrestler B's head ("snaps" it), blocks an arm with the other hand, and spins behind Wrestler B in the direction of the arm block until he is completely behind Wrestler B. See Figures A, B, and C for the entire sequence.

Wrestler A must use proper hip pressure to force Wrestler B's upper body down to mat. Wrestler A's hands and forearms block Wrestler B's shoulders and stop his penetration. Any opponent stuck in this position quickly becomes exhausted and accessible to a defensive takedown. One goal is to force Wrestler B to put his hands on the mat instead of on the legs.

Coaching Points:

- Begin by having Wrestler B shoot with 50% force and momentum and then increase his effort after each successful snap and spin.

- Wrestler A and Wrestler B should alternate positions with each repetition.

Figure A. Wrestler A controls the head of Wrestler B.

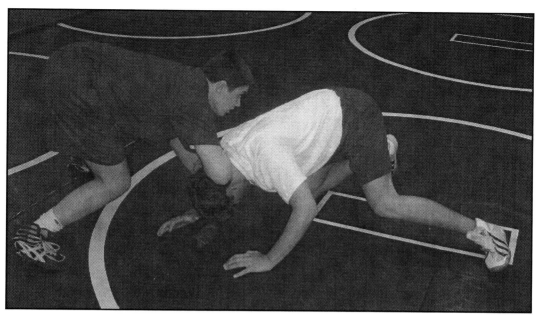

Figure B. Wrestler A snaps down the head of Wrestler B.

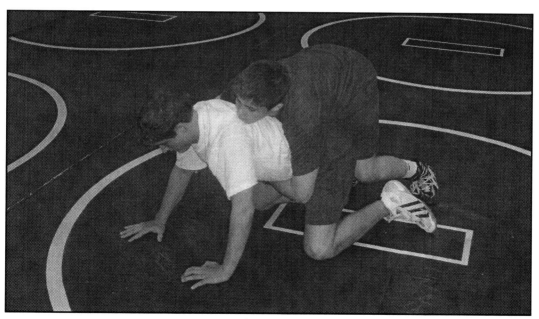

Figure C. Wrestler A spins behind Wrestler B, hip to hip.

Drill #46: Prisoners

Objective: To improve the reaction response to an opponent's quick leg attack

Location: Wrestling room

Description: This drill resembles the snap and spin drill (Drill #45) in that Wrestler A must sprawl, snap the head of Wrestler B, and spin behind after Wrestler B shoots at his legs. This drill is termed Prisoners because Wrestler A must begin in a square or staggered stance, but with his hands on his head, like a prisoner (see Figure A). Wrestler A can remove his hands from the top of his head and sprawl only after Wrestler B shoots at his legs (see Figure B). Wrestler A then completes the drill by shoving hard down on Wrestler B's head, blocking an arm, and spinning behind. Then Wrestler B becomes the prisoner.

A variation to this drill is tap and counter, in which Wrestler A has his back to Wrestler B, who chooses an angle, taps the back of Wrestler A, and then shoots at his legs (see Figure C). Wrestler A must keep his back to Wrestler B until he feels the tap on his back. At that point he can turn, sprawl, and counter the leg attack from Wrestler B.

Coaching Point:

- Remind the wrestlers to keep moving during the drill (left, right, back, forward)—they cannot remain motionless while waiting for Wrestler B to shoot. Wrestler B can shoot at any time and from any angle. In fact, as Wrestler A gains proficiency at the drill, have Wrestler B increase the efforts on his shots from 50% up to 90%.

Figure A. Starting position

Figure B. Wrestler A sprawls after Wrestler B shoots at his legs.

Figure C. Starting position for Tap and Counter

5

Drills for the Top Position

Success at offensive wrestling from the top position depends largely on pressuring the defensive wrestler's upper body so he is forced to keep weight on his hands, controlling his hips so he cannot execute a stand-up or sit-out, and attempting pin holds so he becomes more concerned about staying off his back than escaping. Ultimately, effective wrestling technique from the top position can exhaust the bottom wrestler, lessening his chance for scoring points offensively in the match. The drills in this chapter are designed to teach wrestlers how to maintain correct position and proper pressure when riding the bottom wrestler—and how to pin him.

Drill #47: Froggy

Objective: To practice using the force of the hips and upper body to drive an opponent off his base

Location: Wrestling room

Description: Wrestler A should position his chest tight against the side of Wrestler B, like a frog with bent legs, bent arms, and the head up. One hand should be on Wrestler B's hip and the other should be on his shoulder. Wrestler A is only permitted to use the power of his hips and legs to shove Wrestler B off his base. The arms are used only for balance.

Begin with Wrestler B giving about 50% resistance and have him increase resistance as Wrestler A shows proficiency as the drill progresses. Also, have the two wrestlers switch positions after several repetitions.

Coaching Point:

- Remind wrestlers that they are not allowed to use their arms to push or pull the bottom wrestler off his base. They must learn to rely on the power they can generate from their legs and hips.

Drill #48: Spin to Pin

Objective: To teach wrestlers how to identify pin hold opportunities from a variety of angles and positions when riding

Location: Wrestling room

Description: Begin with Wrestler B on all fours in a regular base position (hands and knees on the mat) and Wrestler A on top with his chest on Wrestler B's back and his hands on top of Wrestler B's shoulders and/or back. On the first whistle, Wrestler A begins spinning around the body of Wrestler B. On the second whistle, Wrestler A puts in a pin hold (e.g., spiral, cradle) and takes Wrestler B to his back.

Coaching Point:

- Though the drill begins with speed (spinning), Wrestler A must be under control and use correct technique when applying his pin hold.

Drill #49: Jam

Objective: To practice proactive wrestling from the top position. The top wrestler must learn to initiate pressure on the bottom wrestler immediately on the referee's whistle and throughout the period when riding.

Location: Wrestling room

Description: Place Wrestler B in a base position and Wrestler A on top in a legal starting position. On the whistle, Wrestler A must drive his chest and hips hard onto the upper torso of Wrestler B, forcing Wrestler B to put weight on his hands and potentially collapse to the mat. Wrestler A can then shift his position from side to side to maintain that pressure and to continue "jamming" Wrestler B (see photo). Wrestler A is permitted to pull or sweep either of Wrestler B's arms as he pressures him.

Coaching Point:

- Be ready to caution wrestlers who jam the bottom wrestler and then relax. The force Wrestler A exerts on the bottom wrestler must be constant from the first to the last whistle.

Drill #50: Pin at the Boundary (Turn His Head)

Objective: To teach how to maintain a tight pin hold and prevent an opponent from using the out-of-bounds line to avoid getting pinned

Location: Wrestling room

Description: Begin with Wrestler A with a half nelson or cradle pin hold on Wrestler B, who must have his head inches away from the boundary line (see Figure A). On the whistle, Wrestler B must push off his feet with the intention of getting himself out of bounds (and out of danger of being pinned). Wrestler A must drive off his feet to turn Wrestler B's upper body and head away from the boundary line and back toward the center of the mat (see Figure B). Wrestler B will then find himself pushing himself back toward the center.

Coaching Points:

- Be sure Wrestler A has a tight pin hold and that he does not lose control as Wrestler B begins pushing and rocking to get out of the pin hold. A potential fall could be lost if an opponent can push himself out of bounds.

- It is also important that Wrestler A be perpendicular to Wrestler B, and that he has his feet away from Wrestler B's feet.

Figure A. Starting position

Figure B. Wrestler A has turned Wrestler B's head away from the boundary.

Drill #51: Float

Objective: To practice riding an opponent who frequently sits out or hip heists from the bottom position

Location: Wrestling room

Description: On the whistle, the offensive wrestler (Wrestler A) follows Wrestler B's sit out motion by staying hip to hip and feet to feet until he hears the whistle again. The wrestlers should change positions after each repetition. Wrestler A should never place his head over the shoulder of Wrestler B or drop his head too low to the mat.

Coaching Point:

- This drill focuses on quickness and reaction, so slower or less-agile wrestlers may experience difficulty trying to "float" with a quicker partner. In such situations, instruct Wrestler B to not move as fast.

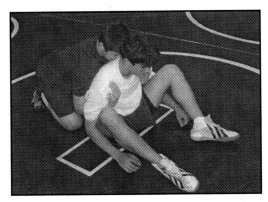

Figure A. Wrestler A is behind Wrestler B with underhooks.

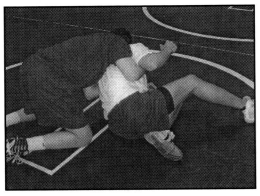

Figure B. As Wrestler B begins to sit out, Wrestler A follows him.

Drill #52: Wrist and Shift

Objective: To develop techniques to maintain control of a bottom wrestler who has been broken down to his belly

Location: Wrestling room

Description: Wrestler A, who is on top, has both hands beneath Wrestler B's armpits and control of one wrist. Wrestler A should be on one side of Wrestler B's body, and Wrestler B's belly should be flat on the mat. If Wrestler A is on the left side of Wrestler B, he should use his left hand to control Wrestler B's right wrist. Wrestler B's chest should be elevated somewhat and his head should be up (see Figure A). On the whistle, Wrestler B begins shifting his hips and moving his arms, forcing Wrestler A to switch wrist control and sides (see Figure B). Continue the drill until Wrestler A has been forced to switch sides at least four or five times, and then have the wrestlers change positions.

Coaching Point:

* Although shifting sides, Wrestler A must never take the pressure off Wrestler B. Wrestler B must also work his wrist free before Wrestler A grabs the opposite wrist and changes sides.

Figure A. Starting position

Figure B. Wrestler A shifts to the other side.

Drill #53: Kick Him Out

Objective: To teach the proper procedure for releasing an opponent when in the top position and to gain confidence in achieving a takedown after doing so under time limitations

Location: Wrestling room

Description: Wrestlers must begin in the optional starting position (see photo). On the whistle, the offensive wrestler (Wrestler A) pushes the upper hip of the defensive wrestler (Wrestler B) down and away and then circles away, immediately preparing to set up a takedown. The wrestlers should change positions after each repetition.

Coaching Point:

- Caution Wrestler A about releasing Wrestler B and staying motionless—or worse, charging at Wrestler B after releasing him. This action could invite Wrestler B to hit a leg attack before Wrestler A can set up his own.

Drill #54: Pin or Kick

Objective: To practice time management for competitions when the top wrestler needs points in a hurry and must either turn the bottom wrestler to gain near fall points or release the bottom wrestler, sacrificing a one-point escape to achieve a potential takedown.

Location: Wrestling room

Description: Begin the drill with Wrestler A on top, controlling a wrist or using his favorite ride. On the whistle, Wrestler A must either turn Wrestler B or release him and attempt a takedown immediately. Wrestler B should begin by offering 60% resistance and increase his resistance up to 90% with each successive turn by Wrestler A.

Coaching Point:

- You have several options for how to lead this drill. You can allow Wrestler A to decide whether to pin or kick, call out "Kick him out!" to Wrestler A at any time, adjust the score to mandate whether Wrestler A should release Wrestler B, or call out "stalling!" to prompt Wrestler A to release Wrestler B.

Drill #55: 30 Seconds

Objective: To improve time management, especially for the 30-second tiebreaker common in scholastic wrestling

Location: Wrestling room

Description: Begin with Wrestler B on his base and Wrestler A on top in a legal starting position. On the whistle, Wrestler A must ride Wrestler B and not get called for stalling or allow an escape. Wrestler B should attempt to escape while giving 80 to 90% effort. After the 30 seconds are up, the wrestlers should change positions.

Coaching Points:

- Coaches should review the situations that typically prompt officials to call stalling on top wrestlers and then monitor their wrestlers throughout the drill, calling out "stalling" whenever it is warranted.

- You can adjust the drill time to 20 or 10 seconds, or even challenge both wrestlers to score points to break the tie.

Drill #56: Stand and Single

Objective: To practice a single-leg takedown against an opponent who hits a clean stand-up

Location: Wrestling room

Description: This drill has two variations. It can begin with Wrestler B on his feet and Wrestler A behind him with his arms locked around Wrestler B's waist. On the whistle, Wrestler A allows Wrestler B to break his grip, but before Wrestler B can turn away, Wrestler A drops quickly to a single-leg takedown, lifts Wrestler B's nearest leg, and finishes the single-leg takedown.

The second option is to begin with Wrestler B on the mat on his base and Wrestler A on top in a legal starting position. On the whistle, Wrestler A allows Wrestler B to stand up, but before Wrestler B can break free entirely, Wrestler A drops quickly to a single-leg, lifts Wrestler B's nearest leg, and finishes the single-leg takedown. Have the wrestlers change positions after each repetition.

Coaching Point:

- The drill assumes that the top wrestler is confronted by a quicker, faster opponent who is especially skilled at hitting a stand-up. Though that type of opponent may easily get to his feet, this does not mean that he can complete his escape. This drill prepares the top wrestler for such a situation.

6

Drills for the Bottom Position

Wrestling from the defensive (bottom) position can be viewed as an advantage for wrestlers who see the bottom as an easy opportunity to score a one-point escape or a two-point reversal. For the wrestler who has strong hips, proficiency with a stand-up or sit-out, or a special maneuver that leads to a reversal, the bottom position can be advantageous.

Drills and techniques from the bottom position must be worked at consistently because even the better wrestler will be on the bottom at some point. Therefore, the drills in this chapter are designed to teach wrestlers how to maintain correct position when on the bottom and to pressure the offensive wrestler into giving up the escape or reversal.

Drill #57: Hip Heisting

Objective: To practice moving the hips up and away from the top wrestler

Location: Wrestling room

Description: Each wrestler begins sitting on the mat with his legs bent, knees up, and arms tight to his sides with his hands on the mat (see Figure A). On the whistle, each wrestler slides one leg (it does not matter which leg he chooses) under the other, pushes off his hands (see Figure B), and moves to a position in which his weight is on the knees. The hands must come off the mat, and the back must be straight up and down.

Coaching Point:

* The hip heist movement needs to be as quick as possible, and the wrestler must have his back straight, head up, and arms bent at his sides at the end of this maneuver.

Figure A. Starting position

Figure B. The wrestler slides one leg under and turns his hips.

Drill #58: Back-Back

Objective: To emphasize back pressure from the bottom position. Strong back pressure is crucial to completing a stand-up and escaping from the bottom, yet too many wrestlers are unaccustomed to moving backward skillfully. This drill helps them master proper back pressure (i.e., pushing their back into the top wrestler) and hip position.

Location: Wrestling room

Description: Wrestler A begins by placing his back against the side of Wrestler B (see photo) and then, on the whistle, uses the power of his legs and hips to shove him around their practice circle. It is important that Wrestler A's hips stay beneath him, that he does not put his hands on the mat, and that he does not become extended. After a short duration, the wrestlers should change positions.

Coaching Point:

• Do not allow the wrestlers simply to lean on their drill partner or put their palms on the mat for more than two seconds.

Drill #59: Find the Hands

Objective: To practice getting hand control of the offensive (top) wrestler. This technique is mandatory for any wrestler who wants to escape from the bottom. This drill enables wrestlers to locate and gain control of the top wrestler's hands by sensing them on various spots on his upper torso or legs, and without having to look for them.

Location: Wrestling room

Description: On the whistle, the offensive (top) wrestler can slide his hands to grab an ankle, tighten his grip on the defensive man's waist, or reach for a wrist. Wherever the top wrestler puts his hands, the bottom wrestler must grab them either at the fingers or wrist. As the bottom wrestler seeks the hands he must also square his hips to the top wrestler and pressure into him. He must learn how to readjust his position to get hand control and complete his original escape.

Coaching Points:

- Tell the top wrestlers not to put their hands in unusual places like behind or on top of the bottom wrestler's head. They must put their hands where they actually would during competition.

- You can eventually add an entire escape technique (e.g., stand-up), but initially the bottom wrestler only needs to move his hips out and find the hands.

Drill #60: Post a Foot

Objective: To teach how to maintain balance and exert proper pressure against the top wrestler with at least one foot posted on the mat

Location: Wrestling room

Description: Wrestler A begins with one knee down, the other foot posted (alternate these throughout the drill), and the back straight, head up, and arms tight to his sides. You can, if desired, grant Wrestler A control of one of Wrestler B's hands. On the whistle, Wrestler B tries to shove or pull Wrestler A off balance. Wrestler A must keep at least one foot posted and eventually rotate off the down knee to post both feet. After a short duration, the wrestlers should change positions.

Coaching Points:

- Wrestler A must keep his body square to Wrestler B, who will be trying to get an angle on him.
- It is important that Wrestler A keeps back pressure on Wrestler B (Back-Back, Drill #58).

Drill #61: Stay Square

Objective: To teach techniques to prevent the offensive (top) wrestler from getting an angle and driving the bottom wrestler to his belly on the mat

Location: Wrestling room

Description: Begin with Wrestler A on his butt and Wrestler B behind him on his knees with his head behind Wrestler A's head. Wrestler B can control no more than one wrist with one hand and grip outside Wrestler A's other elbow with his other hand. On the whistle, Wrestler B attempts to get an angle on Wrestler A by moving from one side to the other while pushing and pulling on Wrestler A. Wrestler A must continually shift his position so that his back is always square to Wrestler B. After a short duration, the wrestlers should change positions.

Coaching Point:

- Remind Wrestler A not to put his palms on the mat (for balance or to push off) for more than two seconds. Also, his palms should only be on the mat when Wrestler B's hands are high on his body.

Drill #62: Wall Stand-Ups

Objective: To develop proper technique and form when completing a stand-up

Location: Wrestling room

Description: Begin with the wrestlers in a legal bottom base position with their backs to a padded wall. On the whistle, the wrestlers post a foot (be sure they all move the same foot) directly in front of them, shove their backs to the wall, and bring their elbows tight to their sides, hands ready to grab the imaginary hands of the opponent on top. Their backs should hit with a solid thud (see photo). They then return to the original starting position, ready to stand up again.

Coaching Point:

*   To add explosiveness to the initial motion, tell the wrestlers to bend their arms somewhat so they can push off their hands with more momentum.

Final position

Drill #63: Pop-Ups

Objective: To improve explosiveness on a stand-up and increase leg and hip strength. This drill can also be used to develop stamina and endurance in the muscles in the legs and arms.

Location: Wrestling room

Description: Begin with the wrestlers in a legal bottom base position and be sure they have at least four to five feet of distance from their teammates (see Figure A). On the whistle, the wrestlers must quickly go from the base position to a solid square stance (i.e., they "pop" up from the mat to their feet) (see Figure B). The wrestlers move from their base position to a stance position in one, quick movement. Constant repetition is necessary when performing this drill.

Coaching Point:

- As the drill progresses, it is not uncommon for wrestlers to tire and begin to neglect a proper stance when on their feet. Instead, they may straighten their legs, bend at the waist, and/or dip their heads. Be sure they maintain a proper stance when on their feet.

Figure A. Starting position

Figure B. Final position

Drill #64: Elevation

Objective: To develop techniques to avoid getting returned to the mat after a stand-up. Completing a stand-up escape depends on the bottom wrestler going from a base position to his feet—and staying there. However, when a wrestler gets to his feet, regardless of his quickness, his opponent can lift him and return him to the mat. Wrestlers, therefore, must remain alert to the possibility of being lifted off the mat. This drill prepares wrestlers for this situation and teaches them how to readjust to complete the original stand-up.

Location: Wrestling room

Description: This drill has two variations. The first version begins with Wrestler A standing and Wrestler B behind him with his arms locked around his waist. On the whistle, the offensive wrestler (Wrestler B) lifts Wrestler A off the mat. Wrestler A lifts his knees to his chest and gets his hips beneath him (see Figure A), waits for Wrestler B to return him to the mat, lands like a cat in the base position, and pops immediately back up into a stand-up, getting hand control when Wrestler B releases his grip. After several repetitions, the wrestlers should change positions.

The second version begins with Wrestler A standing and Wrestler B behind him with his arms locked around his waist. On the whistle, the offensive wrestler (Wrestler B) starts to lift Wrestler A off the mat. Wrestler A hooks in by placing one foot around the calf or ankle of Wrestler B with the laces toward the leg. Wrestler B should then be unable to lift Wrestler A (see Figure B). After several repetitions, the wrestlers should change positions.

Coaching Point:

- For both versions, be sure Wrestler A is also using his hands to maintain his balance and get hand control.

Figure A. Wrestler A brings his knees to his chest

Figure B. Wrestler A hooks in with his left foot

Drill #65: Break the Grip

Objective: To teach the importance of hand control when attempting any escape from the bottom

Location: Wrestling room

Description: This drill has two variations. The first version begins with Wrestler A with one knee down and one foot posted. Wrestler B is positioned behind him holding a tight waist with one hand, and the other hand gripping outside one elbow of Wrestler A. On the whistle, Wrestler A fights to prevent Wrestler B from locking his hands and keeping him on the mat. Wrestler A can, of course, push off his feet and stand while fighting for hand control (see photo). After several repetitions, the wrestlers should change positions.

The second version begins with Wrestler A standing on both feet with slight back pressure on Wrestler B, who has his hands already locked around the stomach of Wrestler A. On the whistle, Wrestler A breaks the grip of Wrestler B by shoving down hard with both hands on the thumb of one of Wrestler B's hands until the pressure breaks Wrestler B's grip. Wrestler A should then swivel his hips and square off against Wrestler B. After several repetitions, the wrestlers should change positions.

Coaching Point:

*   Tell Wrestler B to offer 50% resistance (when locking his hands) at the outset, and increase to 90% resistance at the drill progresses.

Drill #66: Bridge Him Off

Objective: To develop techniques to avoid getting pinned and to increase the endurance and strength in the neck muscles

Location: Wrestling room

Description: Begin with Wrestler A flat on his back and Wrestler B perpendicular to him with his chest resting across the chest of Wrestler A (see photo). On the whistle, Wrestler A must hit a high bridge, suddenly drop his back down to the mat, slide one arm (it does not matter which) into the space created between the two bodies by the sudden drop, and then swivel his chest to the mat, ready to get to a base position. Have the wrestlers change positions after each repetition.

Coaching Point:

- Remind Wrestler B that his only obligation during this drill is to make Wrestler A carry his weight. He should not attempt any pin hold.

Drill #67: Fight the Nelson

Objective: To teach techniques to avoid getting pinned or turned by a half nelson

Location: Wrestling room

Description: Begin with Wrestler A on his belly and Wrestler B with his left hand in a half nelson (he should alternate hands with each repetition). On the whistle, Wrestler A must crank down with his left shoulder, raise his head and chest, use both hands to grab Wrestler B's left wrist, and pull the hand off his neck (see photo). Wrestler A should finish with Wrestler B's left hand planted on the mat and be ready to slide up into a base position. The wrestlers should change positions only after several repetitions have been attempted on both sides.

Coaching Points:

- You can have Wrestler A move to a base position, even a stand-up, after completing the technique. The bottom line, however, is to get free of the half nelson.

- Remind Wrestler B to begin with 50% effort at the outset and increase it to 90% as the drill progresses.

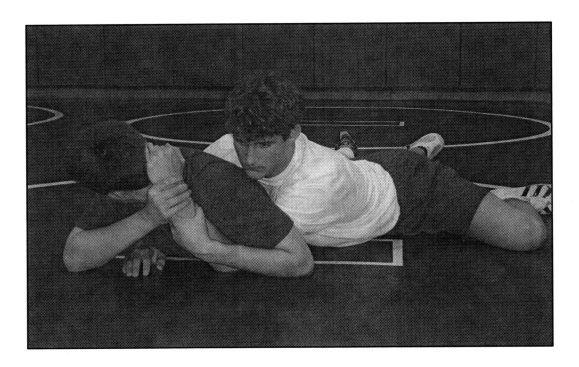

Drill #68: Five Seconds

Objective: To prompt the bottom wrestler to stay on his feet and not get returned to the mat

Location: Wrestling room

Description: Begin with Wrestler A and Wrestler B in a legal, starting, down position. On the whistle, Wrestler A must stand up and stay on his feet for five consecutive seconds. Typically, begin by having this drill last 15 seconds and then gradually decrease to 10 seconds as the drill progresses. A full escape is preferred but not mandatory. Wrestler A must simply stay on his feet for five consecutive seconds during the 10- to 15-second interval.

Coaching Point:

• Both wrestlers give 100% effort during this drill, which can be a game with points awarded to each wrestler.

7

Endurance, Stamina and Strength Drills

Young athletes have to be told that getting in shape means experiencing various levels of discomfort. No one likes to work to exhaustion, yet wrestling does require daily doses of fatigue. Coaches probably have discovered that working their wrestlers too hard in practice discourages some kids, but working them too lightly leaves them physically unprepared for competitions. Is there a happy medium?

The answer is yes. Wrestlers can find practice to be an enjoyable and enriching experience and still work their hardest, regardless of difficulty, if coaches follow these 10 tips:

- Use a variety of drills, competitive games, and scrimmage situations.
- List examples of matches in which an athlete's physical conditioning resulted in victory.
- Point out how tapping into physical reservoirs of energy produces power.
- Reward hustle and diligence both individually and collectively (i.e., provide incentives).
- Have the team pretend that today's practice is the last one of the season.
- Identify those wrestlers who work their hardest. Give them leadership positions.

- Never coach in anger or use physical conditioning activities, like sprints, as punishment.
- Begin and end on time.
- Remind the team that hard work beats talent when talent doesn't work very hard.
- Know when to push them and when to call it a day.

Most often, the wrestler who has physically prepared the hardest in practice triumphs in competition. Nevertheless, some wrestlers may still grumble or groan during an exhausting practice and forget the benefits of hard training. Instead of scolding them, redirect their efforts to a new drill, a competitive game ("Who can get the most takedowns in 30 seconds?" "Which group can total the most chin-ups?"), or a new situation (top vs. bottom, bottom winning by one).

Present videotapes of matches in which one wrestler's superior stamina resulted in his victory, and teach that fatigue in practice is the prerequisite to power in matches. Consider the incentives you can provide for extra effort. For example, give coupons that are donated by the owners of their favorite stores or restaurants in the community. Name your hardest-working upperclassmen as captains, even if they are honorary or temporary positions. Also, never use a strenuous activity (e.g.., sprints, push-ups, leg lifts) as punishment because the wrestlers may equate getting in shape with getting punished, and that is, of course, a connection you don't want them to make.

Finally, be observant and recognize that sluggish effort may be the result of some psychological distraction—that the athletes don't mean to be lazy, but they just can't get focused completely on the tasks at hand. Be ready for such days and have an alternative plan ready. In such a scenario, replace drilling, technique instruction, and wrestling with a series of exercises, agility drills, and/or running. Be creative—have them do yoga, shadowboxing, or aerobics.

Former Major League owner Walter O'Malley bragged once about his Dodger teams, "We're good because we work harder than anybody else." His message is clear and to the point. The challenge is to prompt athletes to identify hard work in practice as the key requirement to success in matches. Hopefully, the aforementioned 10 tips and the drills that follow can help you achieve that goal.

Drill #69: Step-Ups

Objective: To improve leg strength and overall endurance (cardiovascular conditioning)

Location: Gymnasium bleachers

Description: The wrestlers should start with their feet on the gym floor, facing the first bleacher seat. On the whistle, they must continually step up and down onto the bleachers with one foot and then the other. The up-and-down action must continue without stopping until they hear a second whistle. Vary the duration of the drill (e.g., 10, 20, 30, or 60 seconds).

Coaching Point:

- Remind the wrestlers to maintain a position with the legs and arms bent and a vertical back. Caution them, especially the heavier wrestlers, about leaning into the bleachers or getting hunched over. They can put their hands onto the bleachers in front of them for balance but must not lean on them.

Drill #70: Relay Races

Objective: To increase cardiovascular endurance and improve leg strength

Location: Wrestling room, gymnasium, or hallway

Description: Place the wrestlers in lines of three or four against one wall of the wrestling room or gymnasium. This drill consists of simply running to one designated line (either a boundary line already on the mat or gym floor or one designated by athletic tape), touching it with a foot or hand, and then sprinting back to the next wrestler in line, who continues the relay.

Coaching Points:

- You should form groups of various wrestlers (i.e., mixing low, middle, and heavier weights) and formulate some type of incentive for the winning group—for example, allowing them time off at the end of practice.

- You can expand this drill to include bear crawls, crab walks, duck walks, or skipping. Be sure that groups are small (two to four wrestlers) to minimize inactivity.

Drill #71: Weight Class Races

Objective: To increase cardiovascular endurance and improve leg strength

Location: Outside in a park, on the track, in the wrestling room, in the gymnasium, or through school hallways

Description: This drill is a distance-running activity. Break the team up into divisions based on their weight classes. Team A can consist of the boys in weight classes 103, 119, 130, 140, 152, 171, and 215, while Team B has wrestlers in the weight classes 112, 125, 135, 145, 160, 189, and HWT. You award points based on the order of finish, with the first place finisher getting one point, the second place earning two points, etc., until the last wrestler crosses the line. The team with the fewest points is the winner.

Coaching Points:

- You may have to adjust the teams based on the number of wrestlers on the team and the weight classes they occupy.

- You can vary the type of running, including sprints, distance running, bleacher steps, and jogging. When using distance running, begin with a one-mile run on the first day and work toward four to five miles by the sixth week.

Drill #72: Bleacher Steps

Objective: To increase cardiovascular endurance and improve leg strength

Location: Football stadium or gymnasium bleachers

Description: Begin with wrestlers on the bottom step of the bleachers. On the whistle, they must sprint to the top and jog back down.

Coaching Points:

- Tell the wrestlers to keep their eyes on the bleacher steps to avoid stumbling or tripping.
- A variation of this drill is a hill run, in which wrestlers run up and down a steep hill approximately 30 to 100 yards long.

Drill #73: Carry Your Group

Objective: To increase cardiovascular endurance and improve leg strength

Location: Wrestling room, gymnasium, or hallway

Description: Divide the wrestlers into groups of four. Each wrestler must carry the other members of his group one at a time on his back to a spot designated by the coach (usually the other side of the mat or gymnasium). Each wrestler must carry each member once, sprinting the entire way, deposit him at the designated spot, and then sprint back to get the next member of his group. Once he has carried each member of his group to the other side of the room, he must bring each back to the original starting point before the next wrestler begins his turn.

Coaching Points:

- Once again, you may have to be flexible in how you group wrestlers together. Some heavier wrestlers may lack the strength to carry other heavy wrestlers, making this drill useless to them.
- A variation to this drill is partner carries, in which each wrestler carries a single teammate around the mat or gym perimeter, switching off only when the coach signals to do so. Wrestlers should be partnered with a teammate from their own weight class.

Drill #74: Four Corner Sprints

Objective: To increase cardiovascular endurance and improve leg strength

Location: Wrestling room or gymnasium

Description: The wrestlers sprint along the room's longer walls and jog the shorter distances.

Coaching Points:

- As wrestlers tire, they may begin to jog both the long and short distances. Remind them that their speed must increase on the long side of the room or gym.
- This drill can be expanded to include wrestlers doing five to 10 push-ups or sit-ups in every corner before they continue their running.

Drill #75: Short Sprints

Objective: To increase cardiovascular endurance and improve leg strength. Since any wrestling match typically involves rapid adjustments in position and direction, wrestlers need to practice abruptly changing direction and momentum.

Location: Wrestling room or gymnasium

Description: Begin with the wrestlers positioned along one wall. On the whistle, they must sprint to a designated line or spot approximately 15 to 20 feet away and return to the starting point. The duration of each sprint typically is between five and 10 seconds.

Coaching Points:

- The key here is generate speed in one direction and then in another.
- A variation to this drill is to time them (e.g., each wrestler is allowed eight seconds to sprint a certain distance).

Drill #76: Push Pop-Ups

Objective: To increase cardiovascular endurance and stamina in the muscles located in the shoulders, arms, and legs

Location: Wrestling room

Description: Begin with the wrestlers in a standard push-up position. On the whistle, they must push themselves up into a regular square stance. In short, they "pop" from a prone position to a standing one (a square stance).

Coaching Point:

- Be sure the wrestlers have five to six feet separating them from their teammates to prevent any collisions.

Drill #77: Ball Runs

Objective: To increase cardiovascular endurance and improve leg strength

Location: Wrestling room or gymnasium

Description: Place the wrestlers in a single line that stretches in a circle. The lead wrestler must be holding a ball (a volleyball or soccer ball are good choices). On the whistle, the wrestlers begin jogging around the perimeter of the wrestling room or gym and passing the ball down the line. Once the ball reaches the last runner he must sprint to the front of the line with it, become the new leader, and repeat the process until each wrestler has been the leader at least once. If the ball is dropped at any point, the drill starts over and any previous leaders must repeat.

Coaching Point:

- Instruct the leader to slow his speed when the breaks in the line behind him begin to widen.

Drill #78: Team Aerobics

Objective: To improve overall conditioning and aerobic endurance

Location: Wrestling room, gymnasium, or hallway

Description: Wrestlers should form a large circle, but they can also be placed in lines if that is more convenient to your facilities. Begin with the captains and allow each wrestler to announce the aerobic exercise that must be performed for 10 to 15 seconds. These exercises can include push-ups, sit-ups, jumping jacks, squat thrusts, pop-ups, and high knees. Action must be continuous, with no breaks between exercises.

Coaching Point:

• Remind the wrestlers to call out loudly the exercise they select and to step five feet into the circle so their teammates can both hear and see the activity they are to perform.

8

Resistance Training

Most coaches agree that training sessions for wrestlers should include some type of resistance training. Therefore, have each team member lift weights with a partner and chart the poundage on their lifts. You can adopt a variety of approaches to weightlifting, so find an approach that appeals to both you and your wrestlers. Set up a workout schedule that wrestlers can easily follow two or three times each week. Assess their strength at the first workout and then test them at various intervals—for example, at two, six, and 10 weeks.

It is important for wrestlers to recognize how each weightlifting station applies to actual wrestling technique. They must make the connection, for example, between curling a dumbbell and pulling up an opponent's leg. Resistance-training sessions should be as intense as the agility drills and competitive wrestling they do at practice. Coaches must supervise the training sessions carefully and possibly designate when wrestlers move from exercise to exercise.

Views differ regarding the amount of weight athletes should use when resistance training. Allow each wrestler to lift a weight he finds personally challenging in a set of eight to 12 repetitions, unless otherwise noted.

Finally, coaches can also have wrestlers climb ropes and do chin-ups, push-ups, and sit-ups as part of their resistance-training routine. These activities are excellent strength-builders that can be performed if a weightlifting station is unavailable.

Drill #79: Dumbbell and Barbell Curls

Objective: To increase strength and endurance in the muscles of the arm, particularly the biceps. This drill applies specifically to the actions performed when pulling up the leg for a single-leg takedown.

Location: Wrestling room or weight room

Description: The wrestler begins by holding the dumbbells or barbell at thigh level, with the palms facing away from the body about shoulder-width apart. He then curls the weight up to his chest, keeping the elbows tight to his sides and avoiding a rocking motion with his upper body. He should then return the dumbbells/barbell to the original position.

Drill #80: Barbell Squats

Objective: To improve overall body strength and increase the endurance in the thigh and calf muscles. This drill applies specifically to the actions performed for a double-leg takedown and a stand-up.

Location: Wrestling room or weight room

Description: Each wrestler starts by positioning himself underneath the bar so that it sits on his shoulders slightly behind and below the base of his neck. His feet should be slightly wider than shoulder-width apart and his toes should be pointed slightly outward. He then places his hands on the bar slightly wider than shoulder-width apart and looks straight ahead. He performs the drill by taking the barbell off the rack and doing the following:

- Keep the barbell on his shoulders and his grip tight
- Push his hips back slightly as he lowers the weight
- Ensure that his knees do not move past his toes as he squats
- Squat until his thighs are parallel with the floor
- Push up with his legs until he has returned to his original position

Coaching Point:

- Each wrestler should have two spotters, one on each end of the barbell.

Drill #81: Pull-Ups and Chin-Ups

Objective: To improve strength in the muscles of the upper back and arms. This drill applies specifically to the actions performed when riding (wrist ride especially) and performing leg-attack takedowns.

Location: Wrestling room, gymnasium, or weight room

Description: To perform pull-ups, each wrestler begins by gripping the bar above his head with the palms facing away. He pulls himself up until his chin is parallel with the bar and then lowers himself back down slowly and with control. He should continue until he cannot reach the bar with his chin. A chin up involves the same action, except that the wrestler grips the bar with his palms facing toward him.

Coaching Point:

- Be sure the wrestlers reach full extension as they lower themselves.

Drill #82: Dips

Objective: To improve strength in the muscles of the arms, primarily the triceps. This drill applies specifically to the actions performed for a stand-up and when wrestlers are engaged in a stance-and-fight situation in an actual wrestling match.

Location: Wrestling room, gymnasium, or weight room

Description: Each wrestler begins by gripping the handles of the dips apparatus on either side of his chest, raising himself off the floor, bending his knees, and then lowering himself until his arms are at 90-degree angles. He then pushes himself up until his arms are straight.

Coaching Point:

- Heavier wrestlers may struggle to lift themselves off the floor and may need some assistance from a spotter holding their legs below the knees.

Drill #83: Bench Press

Objective: To improve strength in the chest (i.e., the pectoral muscles). This drill applies specifically to the actions performed for a double-leg takedown, upper-body throw, and a stand-up (pushing the chest off the mat).

Location: Weight room

Description: The bench press is probably the most commonly known strength-training exercise. The wrestler lies down with his back on a bench and grips a barbell with his hands at, or slight wider than, shoulder-width. He lowers the barbell to his chest, aiming to touch below his pectorals at the base of his sternum. His hands should be directly above his elbows at this point. He completes the exercise by driving the barbell straight up until the arms are fully extended.

Coaching Points:

- Caution wrestlers about using too much weight because some may think that is the true way to build strength. Instead, they should use a weight they can successfully lift six to 12 times with good form.

- Other effective exercises for the chest include the incline bench press and dumbbell flies, which in some ways duplicate the double-leg takedown.

Drill #84: Upright Row

Objective: To improve strength in the shoulder and arm muscles. This drill applies specifically to any lifting of the opponent done during a match (e.g., a single-leg takedown).

Location: Wrestling room

Description: The wrestler stands holding the barbell or curl bar at thigh level with his hands eight to 12 inches apart and his palms facing toward his body. He pulls the bar toward his chin, leading with his elbows and keeping the bar as close to his body as possible. He then lowers the bar to the original position.

Coaching Point:

- Other effective work on the shoulders and arms include the military press, lateral and front raises with dumbbells, and shrugs.

Drill #85: Rope Climbs

Objective: To improve strength in the muscles of the upper back and arms. This drill applies specifically to the actions performed when setting up a takedown (grip strength), pulling in a single leg, riding (gripping a wrist or tight waist), and pinning.

Location: Wrestling room, gymnasium, or weight room

Description: Wrestlers should pull themselves up the rope using a hand-over-hand approach and gripping the rope with their legs as needed.

Coaching Points:

- Heavier wrestlers often struggle to climb the rope, so encourage them to climb as high as possible.
- Have a spotter loosely hold the bottom of the rope to prevent it from swaying around the room.

Drill #86: Power Course

Objective: To improve the overall cardiovascular endurance of wrestlers and add stamina to all muscle groups. The Power Course offers an intense form of conditioning, a different format for building strength and endurance, and an effective method for evaluating your athlete's stamina.

Location: Wrestling room or gymnasium

Description: The Power Course can consist of various stations (determine the exact number based on the total number of wrestlers) located in the wrestling room and/or gymnasium. On each whistle, the wrestlers move without rest from station to station until each one has completed the circuit two or three times. A typical sequence involves 15 to 30 seconds at each station. Typical stations include pull-ups, rope climbs, sprints, sit-ups, step-ups on bleachers, squat thrusts, high knees, and push-ups.

Coaching Points:

- You have the flexibility to create a Power Course that includes dumbbells and other available weightlifting equipment as desired.
- Wrestlers must at least jog when instructed to go from one station to the next.

9

Competitive Wrestling Drills

Detailed organization is required when leading competitive wrestling drills. You can decide, for instance, if you prefer your team to concentrate on leg attacks or counters from the neutral position and then plan the drills accordingly. The drills featured in this chapter are common ones that coaches will find useful for all wrestling programs—from youth to college. You would be wise to vary the competitive wrestling drills you use, as well as the way you group the athletes, so that the wrestlers do not become stale or slow. Finally, supervise wrestlers closely so they are not colliding with other groups or becoming frustrated or angry with teammates. Do not be afraid to stop all activity to instruct the entire team about what wrestlers should do in a certain situation you observed during competitive wrestling.

Drill #87: Round Robin Wrestling

Objective: To practice wrestling techniques and maneuvers associated with the neutral position

Location: Wrestling room

Description: Group wrestlers in any of the following ways and have them wrestle competitively for a specified time in the neutral position according to their number.

Group of Three

- 1 vs. 2 while 3 rests
- 1 vs. 3 while 2 rests
- 2 vs. 3 while 1 rests

Group of Four

- 1 vs. 2 and 3 vs. 4
- 1 vs. 3 and 2 vs. 4
- 1 vs. 4 And 2 vs. 3

Group of Five

- 1 vs. 2 and 3 vs. 4 while 5 rests
- 1 vs. 5 and 2 vs. 3 while 4 rests
- 1 vs. 4 and 2 vs. 5 while 3 rests
- 1 vs. 3 and 4 vs. 5 while 2 rests
- 2 vs. 4 and 3 vs. 5 while1 rests

Group of Six

- 1 vs. 2, 3 vs. 4, and 5 vs. 6
- 1 vs. 5, 2 vs. 3, and 4 vs. 6
- 1 vs. 4, 2 vs. 5, and 3 vs. 6
- 1 vs. 3, 4 vs. 5, and 2 vs. 6
- 2 vs. 4, 3 vs. 5, and 1 vs. 6

Coaching Points:

- You can vary the time duration from 10 to 60 seconds.
- In groups with an even number of wrestlers, allow a 10- to 15-second interval between whistles for wrestlers to find their next partner and get into proper stances.
- Be sure to call out loudly how the numbers are paired and have the wrestlers continue wrestling until they hear the whistle, regardless of when the takedown is achieved.

Drill #88: One-Minute Matches

Objective: To encourage offensive wrestling in the neutral position and improve the wrestlers' overall stamina, focus, and endurance when they are on their feet

Location: Wrestling room

Description: On the whistle, wrestlers wrestle competitively for one minute at a time. Wrestlers compete against the same partner for 11 to 17 minutes, and each pair can choose at any point to take one one-minute break.

Coaching Points:

- One especially positive point about this drill is that it empowers the wrestlers to determine their own break time. It is not uncommon for some pairs to choose not to take a break at all. Commend wrestlers who do that.

- Always have the number of matches be an odd number—11, 13, 15, or 17.

- A variation of this drill includes engaging wrestlers in four to eight six-minute matches per practice, giving them short breaks in between. They must pair up with different partners as much as possible.

- Another variation is the drill match, in which wrestlers compete against each other using only 80% resistance, but move and drill at a hurried pace over a specific length of time, typically two-minute periods.

Drill #89: Situation Wrestling—Double vs. Sprawl

Objective: To practice both the offensive and defensive sides of a situation in which one wrestler attempts a double-leg takedown and his partner attempts to counter by sprawling

Location: Wrestling room

Description: Wrestler A begins on one or both knees, his hands behind the knees of Wrestler B, his back straight, and his head tight to the side of Wrestler B—looking as though he stopped just before finishing a double-leg takedown. Wrestler B is on the balls of his feet, with his legs bent at the knees, his upper body resting on the shoulders of Wrestler A, and his hands either free or resting on the shoulders of Wrestler A (see photo). On the whistle, both wrestlers go with 100% effort to either complete the double-leg takedown or sprawl, snap, and spin behind. Be sure they continue wrestling until they hear the next whistle, and then have the wrestlers switch positions.

Coaching Points:

- You can vary the time duration of this drill.
- It is productive to ask the unsuccessful wrestler afterward why he couldn't complete the double- leg takedown or finish the sprawl and spin. Use this moment as an effective teaching tool.

Drill #90: Situation Wrestling—Single vs. Wizzer

Objective: To practice both the offensive and defensive sides of a situation in which one wrestler attempts a single-leg takedown and his partner attempts to counter by using a wizzer

Location: Wrestling room

Description: Wrestler A begins on one or both feet, his hands behind the knee of one leg of Wrestler B, his back straight, and his head tight to the hip of Wrestler B—looking as though he stopped just before finishing a single-leg takedown. Wrestler B is on the balls of his feet, with his legs bent at the knees and one hip resting on the near shoulder of Wrestler A. One of Wrestler B's hands is behind the near armpit of Wrestler A in a near-wizzer position and his other hand can rest on the head of Wrestler A (see photo). On the whistle, both wrestlers go with 100% effort to either complete the single-leg takedown or wizzer and spin behind. Be sure they continue wrestling until they hear the next whistle. Then have the wrestlers switch positions.

Coaching Points:

- You can vary the time duration of the drill.
- It is productive to ask the unsuccessful wrestler afterward why he couldn't complete the single-leg takedown or finish the wizzer and spin behind. Use this moment as an effective teaching tool.

Drill #91: Situation Wrestling—Wrist vs. Belly

Objective: To practice both the offensive and defensive sides of a situation in which the defensive (bottom) wrestler has been forced to his belly and must get to a base position to avoid a stalling call and the offensive (top) wrestler must attempt a pin hold to avoid a stalling call.

Location: Wrestling room

Description: Wrestler A begins on his belly with his forearms in front of his face and angled out. Wrestler B begins on top, angled to one side (not lying on top of Wrestler A), and has control of one wrist (see photo). On the whistle, both wrestlers go with 100% effort. Wrestler A must push himself at least to his base, and Wrestler B must maintain pressure on Wrestler A to keep him on his belly as he looks for a pin hold (e.g., half nelson) opening. Be sure they continue wrestling until they hear the next whistle. Then have the wrestlers switch positions.

Coaching Points:

- You can vary the time duration of the drill.
- It is productive to ask the unsuccessful wrestler afterward why he couldn't complete the half nelson or get to a base position. Use this moment as an effective teaching tool.

Drill #92: Situation Wrestling—Back vs. Pin Hold

Objective: To practice both the offensive (top) technique and defensive (bottom) maneuvers associated with a pinning combination

Location: Wrestling room

Description: Begin with Wrestler B on his back and Wrestler A with a nelson or cradle (see photo). On the whistle, Wrestler B must maneuver to get off his back and Wrestler A must maintain his pin hold and, if possible, pin Wrestler B. Be sure they continue wrestling until they hear the next whistle. After a designated time, have the wrestlers switch positions.

Coaching Points:

- You can vary the time duration of the drill.
- It is productive to ask the unsuccessful wrestler afterward why he couldn't pin his partner or get to a base position. Use this moment as an effective teaching tool.

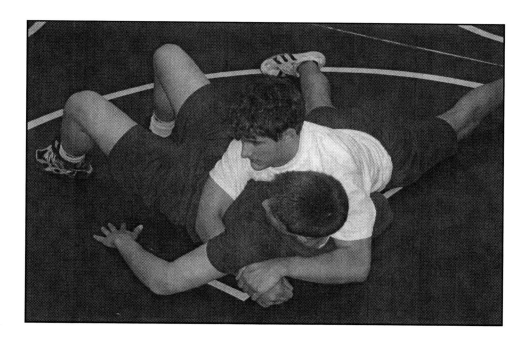

Drill #93: Shuffle in a Circle and Attack

Objective: To encourage offensive wrestling from the neutral position by forcing both wrestlers to step aggressively toward his drill partner and attempt a takedown

Location: Wrestling room

Description: Begin with the wrestlers directly opposite each other on the practice circle in square stances (see photo). On the first whistle, they must begin a slow shuffle in the direction designated by the coach (left or right). On the second whistle, they must step immediately to the center of the circle and attempt a takedown.

Coaching Point:

- Caution wrestlers about butting heads if they charge simultaneously into the center of the practice circle. You certainly want them to be aggressive, but they should not be out of control. They should be in motion and use a set-up before attempting a takedown.

Drill #94: Freestyle Wrestling

Objective: To introduce a freestyle wrestling format and change the tempo and routine of a practice, especially as related to the neutral position

Location: Wrestling room

Description: Begin with the wrestlers in the neutral position and remind them that they cannot allow their backs to be exposed to the mat—ever. On the whistle, they wrestle at 100% effort for the designated time under freestyle rules.

Coaching Point:

- This drill assumes that the wrestlers have at least some knowledge of the rules associated with freestyle wrestling and understand that they should never expose their backs or back up. You should probably have two experienced wrestlers do a brief preview match to expose all team members to the rules and scoring associated with freestyle wrestling.

Drill #95: Greco-Roman Wrestling

Objective: To introduce Greco-Roman wrestling techniques and to alter the format and routine of neutral position wrestling during a practice

Location: Wrestling room

Description: Begin with the wrestlers in the neutral position and remind them that they cannot attempt any leg attacks—only upper-body throws, locks, and sweeps. On the whistle, they wrestle with 100% effort for a designated time.

Coaching Point:

- This drill assumes that the wrestlers have at least some knowledge of the rules associated with Greco-Roman wrestling (or, at least, upper-body techniques). You may show a video or instruct briefly that they must never expose their backs or back up. You should probably have two experienced wrestlers do a brief preview match to expose all team members to the rules and scoring associated with Greco-Roman wrestling.

Drill #96: Counter Wrestling

Objective: To practice techniques associated with countering any offensive technique from the neutral position. Although the focus here is on defensive wrestling, the ultimate goal is to score points (i.e., takedowns) after countering.

Location: Wrestling room

Description: On the whistle, both wrestlers compete with 100% effort with Wrestler B only shooting leg attacks and Wrestler A only countering (e.g., using sprawls, front head locks, wizzers). Wrestler A is not allowed to attempt an offensive takedown. After a designated amount of time, the wrestlers must switch approaches. Also, once a takedown has been achieved, the wrestlers should return to their feet and continue the drill until they hear the whistle.

Coaching Points:

- Although he has been designated as the countering wrestler, Wrestler A is not permitted to back up or avoid contact with Wrestler B.

- Wrestler A can initiate any countering technique (e.g., snap and spin, front headlock) to achieve a takedown.

10

Games

Some coaches avoid using games in practice because they fear their athletes will lose focus or not stay serious about learning techniques. However, playing a fun game during practice can motivate some wrestlers and provide a much-needed distraction for others. A game can truly give a tremendous psychological boost to some athletes. One baseball coach even had an Easter egg hunt out on the diamond that had players running around and scooping plastic egg shells with candy inside. The players ran, laughed, and enjoyed the chocolate and jelly beans. These athletes were still active, but the rigor of practice had been replaced, at least for a short period, by a fun activity.

Games can break the monotony of a practice and offer another type of competitive challenge for athletes, and once you play a game in practice you will probably hear your wrestlers ask to play that game again. Use such a request as a motivator (i.e., if everyone accomplishes a certain task in a set time, you will let them play a game). The wrestlers will probably work their hardest for the opportunity to play that game again. The following games can be performed on the wrestling mat at any point of a practice.

Drill #97: King of the Mat

Objective: To encourage offensive wrestling in the neutral position and to reward wrestlers who aggressively pursue takedowns

Location: Wrestling room

Description: This game involves the entire team in that all members should end up wrestling each other at least once. Begin with each wrestler paired up with a partner who is in or near his weight class. Typically, a 15- to 20-second interval is appropriate before switching partners. Each wrestler tries to accumulate as many takedowns as possible against all opponents. The winner is the wrestler with the most individual takedowns.

It is entirely possible that heavier or more skilled wrestlers will end up paired with lightweights or less skilled athletes. Allow these matchups to take place. While the goal for both wrestlers is to accumulate takedowns, the lighter or less skilled wrestler may simply choose to tie up or counter his opponent to prevent any takedown accumulation. This game involves strategy as well as technique.

Coaching Points:

- Watch for heavier wrestlers continually trying to compete against lightweights.
- Remind wrestlers that they are on the honor system for counting their takedowns.

Drill #98: Touched You Last

Objective: To improve overall conditioning and have fun

Location: Wrestling room or gymnasium

Description: Begin with a captain or team leader being "it" so he must touch any other wrestler, making him the new "it." On the whistle, the wrestlers must run, dodge, and duck whoever is "it" to avoid being the last one touched. Each game should have a set time limit.

Coaching Point:

- Add an incentive, such as extra push-ups or sit-ups for whoever is the last one touched.

Drill #99: Scooter

Objective: To improve overall conditioning and strengthen muscles in the hips and arms

Location: Wrestling room

Description: Form teams that are evenly mixed in terms of weight, talent, and skill level. Except for the first wrestler in line, each team member should be sitting directly behind a teammate and have his legs draped around the wrestler in front of him under his armpits (see photo). On the whistle, the teams must scoot on their butts down the mat without breaking contact with any member of their team. Wrestlers are allowed to use their hands to push off the mat and maintain balance.

Coaching Point:

- If the chain breaks, the wrestlers in front must stop until the other wrestlers on their team have reconnected.

Drill #100: Crab Soccer

Objective: To promote a team concept, work at hip motion, strengthen the arm muscles, and have fun

Location: Wrestling room

Description: As in regulation soccer, wrestlers (with the exception of the designated goalie) are not allowed to use their hands—only their head, chest, and feet. Divide the wrestlers into two teams that begin at either end of the mat. They must be on their butts with their knees bent and their hips beneath them (see photo). Establish penalties for using the hands either by accident or on purpose, along with dimensions for the goals and any out-of-bounds lines. Most often, you can allow the ball to bounce off the wall and still be in play. To begin the game, toss a soccer ball or volleyball into the middle and blow a whistle. Action should continue until a certain score or time limit has been reached.

Coaching Point:

• Coaches should supervise closely to watch for wrestlers kicking each other.

Drill #101: Pull Him Out (of the Circle)

Objective: To build strength in the arms, abdominals, and shoulders

Location: Wrestling room

Description: Pair up wrestlers according to weight class, strength, and skill level and place them back to back in the center of a practice circle. Each pair intertwines their arms so that each wrestler has an underhook and an overhook on his partner (see photo). On the whistle, each wrestler must attempt to pull his partner out of the circle. The first winner is the wrestler who can get his opponent's butt to the edge of the circle.

Coaching Points:

- Check that each wrestler has both an underhook and an overhook (it is unfair to start by having two underhooks).
- Remind the wrestlers to pull, not push, their opponents to the edge of the circle.
- Have a brief time limit (15 to 20 seconds). This game forces wrestlers to work on maintaining balance and to develop the endurance of certain muscle groups.

About the Author

Keith Manos is an English teacher and the former wrestling coach and athletic director at Richmond Heights (OH) High School.

Manos was named Division III Ohio Wrestling Coach of the Year (1988), NE District Division III Wrestling Coach of the Year (1989), GCWCOA Division III Wrestling Coach of the Year (1989), and East Suburban Conference Wrestling Coach of the Year twice (1988 and 1989). The Greater Cleveland Wrestling Coaches and Officials Association honored him with their Award of Merit in 2002. Manos was the head coach of the United States All-Star Wrestling Team (vs. Oklahoma All-Stars) in 1989 and head coach of the Ohio All-Star Wrestling Team in 1991, and has coached multiple all-star wrestling teams and wrestling clubs in Toledo, Sandusky, and Cleveland.

During his tenure as a head coach, Manos had 29 qualifiers to the state tournament, with 21 state tournament placers and three state champions, including Dan Hanson, a four-time state champion. In eight years at Richmond Heights High School, Manos's teams finished in the top 10 at the state tournament five times.

In 2000, Keith was honored as Ohio's English Teacher of the Year by the Ohio Council of Teachers of English and Language Arts. He has published six other books for teachers and coaches.

He lives in Willoughby, Ohio, with his wife, Cheryl, daughter, Brittny, and twin sons, John-Morgan and Christian.